CHI

FOR

CHILDREN

BETTY SUTHERLAND

CHI
FOR
CHILDREN

A Practical Guide to Teaching Tai Chi and Qigong in Schools and the Community

SINGING
DRAGON

LONDON AND PHILADELPHIA

The music in the *Chi for Children* DVD is from 'Tai Chi', from the Lifestyle Series, published by Global Journey Ltd. Used by kind permission of Global Journey Ltd.

First published in 2011
by Singing Dragon
an imprint of Jessica Kingsley Publishers
116 Pentonville Road
London N1 9JB, UK
and
400 Market Street, Suite 400
Philadelphia, PA 19106, USA

www.singingdragon.com

Library of Congress Cataloging in Publication Data
Sutherland, Betty.
  Chi for children : a practical guide to teaching tai chi and qigong in
schools and the community / Betty Sutherland.
    p. cm.
  Includes index.
  ISBN 978-1-84819-055-9 (alk. paper)
  1. Tai chi--Handbooks, manuals, etc. 2. Qi gong--Handbooks, manuals, etc.
I. Title.
  GV504.S867 2011
  613.7'148083--dc22

                    2010049027

British Library Cataloguing in Publication Data
A CIP catalogue record for this book is available from the British Library

ISBN 978 1 84819 055 9

Printed and bound in Great Britain

Every day the teacher repeats those actions that lead to understanding.
Chop wood, carry water, every day. Without routine/repetition there is no
learning. Without surprise there is no wisdom.

Lao Tzu, *Tao Te Ching*

CONTENTS

ACKNOWLEDGEMENTS

My first acknowledgement is to the art of Tai Chi Chuan – without it I wouldn't be here.

Lots of people have helped me on my journey in some way or another, all of whom I am extremely indebted to.

My first big thank you is to my long-suffering husband Dougie, who has been sucked in to the Tai Chi vortex by association. He thinks we're all a bit 'wacky' but supports me enormously and recognizes how beneficial Tai Chi is to me.

I also wish to thank the following people:

My Sifu, Ian Cameron, who was the first person to encourage my studies in the art and continues to do so. His senior students in Edinburgh, Malcolm, Sally and Stephen, who also support and encourage my training (www.five-winds.co.uk).

Sue Dunham of Little Yin Chinese Therapies. Sue has been my 'rock' and is always there for me. Her contribution to this book is greatly appreciated – a true friend (www.littleyin.co.uk).

Northern Legacy, for the video and pictorial footage (www.northernlegacy.org.uk).

Steph Parkin and Jess – hi guys.

Bob France – also known as Bob the Buddha, of the North Yorkshire Qigong Society, with his unique talents in Eastern arts (www.bobfrance.co.uk).

Harewood House, Yorkshire (the beautiful backdrop to the DVD) for the use of their grounds and for their fantastic support (www.harewood.org).

Andy Clay, and the Barlby Sports Partnership (www.barlbyhigh.n-yorks. sch.uk; see DVD).

Dr George Xinsheng Zhang, Director of the School of Oriental and African Studies (SOAS), University of London and London Confucius Institute.

Embsay Primary School, Yorkshire (www.embsay.n-yorks.sch.uk; see DVD).

Helena and Eileen Carter (www.21stcenturychildhood.co.uk; see DVD).

Kirsty Allan and students, Kirk Smeaton Church of England Primary School (www.kirksmeaton.n-yorks.sch.uk).

Oscar Gawron and the Tang Long Kung Fu School (www.tang-long. co.uk).

Paul Hirst and Dr Linda Harris.

Wakefield Healthy Schools (www.wakefield.gov.uk).

Whitley and Eggborough Community Primary School (www.whitley-eggborough.ik.org).

Bill and Debbie Beattie, Potterton Park, Yorkshire.

And, of course, Jessica Kingsley, Lisa and the team at Singing Dragon who have shown confidence in my work and been an unbelievable source of support and guidance – truly a joy to work with (www.singingdragon. com).

Last but not least my mum and dad – who started it all!

ABOUT THE AUTHOR

My name is Betty Sutherland. Like many people I worked in a pressurized environment with deadlines and commitments. Driven by anxiety and by my peers, I started to show physical signs of stress, which developed into serious ill health. After trying the usual 'fixes' to sort this out – complaining to my boss about my workload, taking time out on a beach – eventually I was encouraged to 'take up Tai Chi'.

I was very lucky the day I walked through the door of the Five Winds School of Tai Chi Chuan in Edinburgh and was warmly welcomed by Ian Cameron, who was to become my Sifu (teacher).

Ian first studied Tai Chi Chuan with Sifu Cheng Tin Hung in Hong Kong, and has been teaching in the UK since the 1970s. His contribution to Tai Chi in the West is legendary, where he has acquired a reputation as one of the foremost practitioners and teachers of the art in Great Britain.[1]

I study Wudang Tai Chi Chuan (derived from traditional Wu style), and have been a student of the Five Winds School of Tai Chi Chuan in Edinburgh since 1994. I consider myself very fortunate to be able to say that Tai Chi works for me; it was as though I had been looking for it all my life.

Through my studies and practice, I have achieved the grade of Senior Instructor in Tai Chi Forms, Pushing Hands, Martial Applications, Weapon Forms and Internal Strengths.

I am a member of the Tai Chi Union for Great Britain, and listed as an 'A' grade instructor. I am also a member of the British Council for Chinese Martial Arts (BCCMA).

---

1   Source: Sifu Ian Cameron, Five Winds School of Tai Chi Chuan, Edinburgh.

In 2002–03, I competed in the Tai Chi Chuan and Internal Martial Arts European Championship and Festival of Chinese Martial Arts and British Open Tai Chi Championship, winning medals in several disciplines.

My Tai Chi journey has taken me on a varied and rich path, allowing me to participate in events I would never have dreamed of being fortunate enough even to witness. I feel very privileged to be part of the Tai Chi community and to meet fascinating people offering riches beyond anything I had previously imagined. Each and every person I have met throughout this journey has left a fond memory and often a lesson learned.

Throughout this journey the words of my Sifu, Ian Cameron, ring in my ears: 'Tai Chi can change your life, but it takes time!' Tai Chi has definitely changed my life *for the better*, but it does take time, and I intend to practise for a very long time. I'm sure there will always be more to learn.

My Journey Continues

Tai Chi has taken me on a journey of discovery, teaching students of all ages and abilities in schools, clubs, youth groups (Girl Guides and Boy Scouts) and colleges across the UK. Students range from pupils and teachers to traditional Wudang Tai Chi martial artists. Within the healthcare system I have provided Tai Chi training for a range of clients, from doctors and health professionals who are looking at Tai Chi as an 'exercise for non-pharmacological management of anxiety and depression',[2] to the Spinal Injuries Association where I have run seated Tai Chi workshops.

Teaching Children

In 2006 I formed UK Tai Chi Ltd and developed Chi for Children,™ a unique programme of educational Tai Chi/Qigong for schools. This programme has shown that students can improve concentration levels, discipline and application by utilizing techniques from these ancient Chinese arts. Chi for Children has been so successful that we now train teachers to deliver the programme in schools.

---

2   Source: Dr Linda Harris.

ABOUT CHI FOR CHILDREN

Chi for Children is an educational training programme, based on the Chinese arts of Tai Chi Chuan and Qigong, which offers benefits to health, wellbeing and education for students aged 6 to 86.

Thank you for choosing this book – it has been written with you in mind.

- Are you...the teacher who is looking for proven techniques to improve discipline, enhance concentration levels and outcomes in primary aged school children?

- Are you...the activity/youth group leader or teacher of teenage students?

- Are you...the parent or carer who cares about children's physical and mental wellbeing?

Yes? That's right, this book is for *you.*

Within this book you will find the practical tools and techniques to enable you to learn Tai Chi (a Chinese martial art) and Qigong (a Chinese healing art), giving you the necessary skills to teach the programme to a basic level. With this information you will be able to learn short sequences of Tai Chi, called forms, and Qigong exercises for health. Both you and your students will be able to benefit from this valuable form of exercise that's also fun to do.

You will also find some guidance as to the purpose of the exercises and the history behind the techniques.

For further information on Chi for Children, Educational Tai Chi/ Qigong for Schools and Teacher Training, please contact Betty Sutherland, Senior Instructor, UK Tai Chi. E-mail: info@chiforchildren.co.uk, or see my website: www.uktaichi.com.

HOW TO USE THIS RESOURCE

The techniques can be practised in a room, hall or warm garden. Please ensure that the room is clear of any obstacles that you or your students may bump against. Please pay attention to your fitness levels and abilities, and also those of your students. You may wish to carry out health and safety risk assessments to help you identify hazards. For example, you may wish to:

- identify hazards present in the environment, e.g. slippery floors
- identify the people at risk, their health and personal fitness levels, e.g. young people, new/expectant mothers, existing medical conditions
- evaluate the risk, identify and evaluate existing controls
- record the findings
- review the risk assessment regularly.

Being aware of your own abilities is paramount and you must be patient, and allow your learning to develop gradually. Your intention should not be to push yourself or others, to be better/higher/lower or quicker. If we do Tai Chi and Qigong for ourselves the rewards will follow.

To help you learn the complex postures, there are four tutorials. In the format of a book and a DVD, these 'aids to learning' have been specifically designed with clear, easy-to-follow, step-by-step instructions.

They are like Yin and Yang, in that both depend on each other and you need to work with them together to get results. The book tells you 'why you are doing what you are doing' and the DVD shows you the postures. Together they make a resource which has been developed specifically to ease and enhance your learning. Still images of the postures, which are taken from the DVD, are included throughout the book, and the corresponding DVD timing is written along the top right hand edge of each image. Please note that visuals of breathing are not included on the DVD. Please see pages 31–32 for a detailed discussion of breathing.

No special equipment is required, just a pair of flat-soled shoes (plimsolls or flat trainers) and loose, comfortable clothing.

The exercises should be undertaken in a mindful and gentle manner and should never cause discomfort and pain. Should you have any concerns regarding your own or your students' health, please consult a doctor before embarking on these exercises.

To enhance your understanding, please look out for valuable information highlighted with the following symbols:

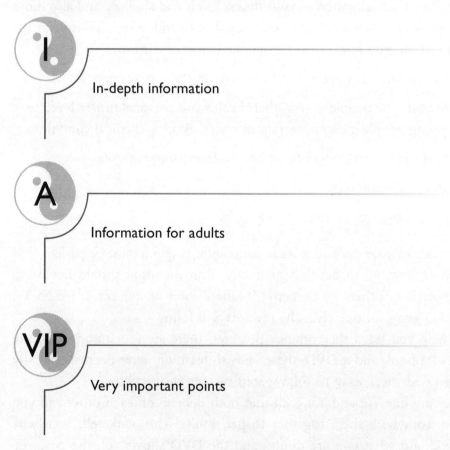

In-depth information

Information for adults

Very important points

The material is based on our unique programme of ancient Chinese arts which I have developed into educational Tai Chi/Qigong – 'Chi for Children'. The programme is currently being delivered in schools by the UK Tai Chi team and teachers.

UK Tai Chi offers an extensive insight into the history and benefits the ancient arts can bring to health, wellbeing and education. Practised this way you will, in time, have an understanding of these ancient arts and gain some of the benefits they can bring. The success of the programme depends on *you!* Your understanding will be all the more powerful and complete through participation.

As you progress through the resource you will meet some challenging postures called the Tai Chi Form (for more on form see note 4 page 23). Although the form is trained in a specific order, each technique and exercise in this resource can be practised 'stand-alone', which is especially useful when you are working on the more complex postures.

INTRODUCTION

The Programme

The programme brings together traditional Wudang Tai Chi and contemporary teaching methods. The material and techniques can be practised from age 6 to 86 (and beyond).[3] However, for the younger age group a story leads the student through the exercises to capture their imagination and ignite their enthusiasm. With continued practice, it becomes an experiential journey that is different every time.

This resource is an *aid to learning*. Although an excellent tool and foundation to future training, to get the most benefit from Tai Chi/Qigong, we recommend that you undertake training with UK Tai Chi. For more information please see www.uktaichi.com.

We talk about teaching Tai Chi as 'laying down sheets of rice paper'. Each sheet is like a sliver of learning; put down one sheet at a time.

After a period of time you will have a thick pile of rice paper and a substantial amount of learning.

---

3   The benefits are the same whatever age you are. However, from experience I have observed that children are alive to the charms of this type of exercise and quickly remember and respond to it.

Encourage your students to help you as you are also 'new to the subject'. Empowering others always produces lots of enthusiasm.

What is Tai Chi?

Tai Chi Chuan (often shortened to Tai Chi) translates to 'supreme ultimate fist', which is represented by the Yin/Yang symbol (see page 26) and is an internal martial art.

Tai Chi Chuan (or Taijiquan) is one of three internal martial arts of China. 'Internal' relates to the fact that you are aware of all aspects of the exercise happening together. That is, the movement, quietness of the mind and breath all come together, making this a truly holistic discipline.

The roots of Tai Chi Chuan are in the martial arts of ancient China and are thought to have originated in the Wudang mountains with the Taoist monk, Chang San-feng (born 1247 AD). Wudang means 'martial duty'. In a violent period of Chinese history and out of a basic need to survive, the martial skills, based on the principle of Yin and Yang, evolved (for more information on Yin/Yang see pages 25–26).

All martial arts are 'disciplines' and this is particularly obvious in Tai Chi when you understand the reason behind the movements. The slow mindful sequence of movements or postures that most people think typical of Tai Chi are, in fact, martial moves (called applications) strung together and practised in sequences called forms. Although this may look similar to dance-like movements, the movements are specific martial applications practised slowly and continuously, almost like a 'Kata' in Karate.[4] Tai Chi has an amazing richness of movement allowing us to learn many different applications. Many are repeated and while everything in Tai Chi is repetition, this is the key to further improvement.

What is Chi?

'When we discipline the body, we discipline the mind.'[5] This is very important as it means that we can 'keep our head' in times of pressure, which is especially worthwhile when others are 'losing' theirs!

Chi translates to 'energy' or 'breath'. However, we should also recognize that the Chi of Tai Chi has a particular significance that it shares with the Qi of Qigong, with Chi and Qi being different ways of expressing the same Chinese character in English. (See Tutorial 1 for more on Chi.)

What is Qigong?

Qigong is an ancient Chinese healing art. Qigong (pronounced Cheegong) translates as 'energy cultivation for health'. Qigong is practised in a series of movements designed to cultivate energy in order to benefit health.

Qigong is part of Traditional Chinese Medicine (TCM) and can be traced back to the legendary Yellow Emperor. Evidence suggests the first forms of Qigong can be linked to meditative practice and gymnastic exercises for health (circa 168 BC), bearing physical resemblance to some of the Qigong exercises that are practised today. Training in Qigong offers a holistic way

---

4   Kata is a Japanese word that translates to 'form'. It is a sequence or pattern of movements practised in martial arts training.

5   Source: Sifu Ian Cameron, Five Winds School of Tai Chi Chuan, Edinburgh.

for us to think about our health in a positive manner and, when practised on a regular basis, may help protect against ill health.

TCM is a complete system, and even today Chinese medicine is used extensively in the East for maintaining good health.

I have not gone into this vast subject in depth in this book. However, where relevant, explanations relating to the benefits from each exercise are highlighted.

Meditation and Mindfulness

Meditation and Mindfulness in Practice

- *Meditation* is the practice of deep thinking or non-thinking, often practised without movement. During practice we endeavour to cultivate a feeling of internal calmness. Tai Chi and Qigong are known as 'meditation in movement'.

- *Mindfulness* is working within the moment. We recognize that during training in Tai Chi and Qigong we are working on a subconscious level, offering the student a feeling of calmness and stillness. Once established we can train ourselves to engage mindfulness at any time during our day.

The importance of a healthy mind cannot be underestimated.

During preparation for Tai Chi the aim is to experience a physical and psychological 'break with the past': to eliminate negativity, stress or fearfulness and replace these negative feelings with positivity, confidence and calmness. It doesn't matter what happened earlier, you cannot change that, or what is going to happen next. However, you can make a difference to what is happening now.

Meditation and mindfulness may not be something we think of as relevant to children, but they will benefit from the quietness that comes with practising Tai Chi and Qigong if it is presented as part of learning. For example, children relate to the idea of reducing the constant chatter in their head. The Chinese call this chatter the 'Manic Monkey' (see Tutorial 1).

The Zone

Once you or your students are in the mindful zone, you will feel the atmosphere within the training room become calm and composed, recognizing that together you have created a good working environment.

Meditation is a holistic discipline during which the practitioner disciplines the mind in order to appreciate the benefits gained by stilling the 'Manic Monkey'.

Meditation is difficult; however, you don't have to sit for 20 minutes with your legs crossed. Start by finding five minutes in your day when you don't have to be thinking, for example, when you are waiting for the kettle to boil. It's not as though you could be doing anything else anyway!

Tai Chi and Qigong have grown from a common root which they share with Chinese medicine. The movements are gentle and apparently effortless, yet they are in fact very powerful and bring tremendous benefits to anyone who adopts them as part of a regular healthcare strategy.

Yin and Yang

As we have already discovered, Tai Chi Chuan translates to 'supreme ultimate fist'. 'Supreme' and 'ultimate' represent the principal of opposites as exemplified in Yin and Yang. The word 'fist' reminds us that we are talking about Chi in a martial way.

In the Yin/Yang symbol, we not only see the distinct nature of opposites, we also see the flexibility that is held within it (the harmony line between the light and dark).

In the Resources at the end of the book you will find templates of the Yin/Yang symbol. You could cut out the symbol in order to create a 'spinner'. As the symbol spins you will be able to see 'change' as black turns to white and vice versa.

One important aspect of the Yin/Yang symbol is the line between the black half and the white half. This is called the harmony line.

It is *extremely* important to work with harmony in Tai Chi: harmony with the world, your surroundings and yourself, and even more so with others – friends and family.

Discipline – E-bay

In my experience most children respect the need for discipline when training in Tai Chi. From the outset we establish the guidelines which allow training to continue with mutual goals.

I have seen overall behaviour improve when Tai Chi principles are adopted outside the training room and I think that this is because a key component of any martial art is *discipline*. This discipline of mind and body is an essential part of every Tai Chi class, especially with children.

Used in the Dojo (training hall for martial arts), the word E-bay calls students to *attention*. It is a good tool for bringing everyone into line and letting the students know what you expect of them from the outset.

When you (the Sifu or leader) clap your hands twice it means that you are calling your students to attention. At this sound your students look at you for the next instruction. At the same time they should stamp their feet (left, right), drop their hands to their sides and all say 'E-bay' loudly to show that they are paying attention. Once everyone has had a chance to have a giggle, *silence is expected.*

You can use this at any point during the lesson should you wish to call attention. Most people will have heard of E-bay, although not in this context, and that familiarity is a great help. Also, the fact that they get to make some noise means that they will also enjoy what is, in a roundabout way, an instruction to pay attention!

Respect – Gung Fu

Everyone loves this exercise. I always emphasize that respect for others is an extremely important part of Chinese teaching and this is also reflected in Tai Chi. Being respectful is another quality that has much value outside the Dojo.

At the end of a class, teacher and students should show respect to each other in the form of a physical and vocal acknowledgement.

Gung Fu translates to good or hard work and when said to another is accompanied by the following gesture:

1.   Place a lightly closed right fist into the open palm of the left hand.

2.   Slightly bow, saying as you do so 'Gung Fu'.

3.   Make this gesture between students and teacher and then between each other to show that you respect your partner's hard work.

Note to teacher: ensure students are not standing too close to each other. If they are too close and bow they could bump heads!

Tutorial 4 @ 05.41

Do not confuse Gung Fu (hard work) with Kung Fu, which is a generic name for Chinese martial arts.

Fun, Fun, Fun

The most important element of and outcome from Tai Chi can be summed up in three words: Fun, fun, fun!

This is particularly important when teaching children as it is fun that will keep them engaged and wanting to come back for more. Ask a group of six- to eight-year-olds what they would like to get from your class and the answer will undoubtedly be 'Fun!'

Fortunately, it's not a hard promise to keep because the moves and noises in Qigong and Tai Chi are perfect for inspiring fun and laughter. Also, the level of benefit to young and old alike increases considerably when delivered with that important ingredient.

Remember: keep the fun in to get the most out!

GETTING STARTED

It is important that you are completely focused and engaged before embarking on the more complicated movements.

The following simple warm-up exercises are a lot of fun, but you have to pay attention.

During this section you should allow the students to interact freely with you and their fellow students, particularly during the Chi Brushing, as it will increase their commitment to the lesson and encourage a feeling of anticipation, enjoyment and bonding.

Breathing

Your mental state has a significant effect on breathing and the nervous system. When we are distressed or angry, our breathing becomes shallower and faster, and our heart rate also quickens. Some people may even sigh loudly to empty their lungs and then gasp to take in as much air as possible. This innate reaction is linked to our 'fight or flight' response and can result in hyperventilation, dizziness and in extreme cases fainting, which can create a feeling of anxiety. You may have experienced this at some point.

However, being aware of what is happening to us when we are emotionally challenged can help alleviate the symptoms. The ideal way is to breathe slowly and deeply, through the nose, using the diaphragm muscle, with a feeling of expanding the abdomen and dropping the breath – *do not force* the breath.

This technique is Nasal Breathing. If you suffer from nasal congestion, you or your students can breathe through the mouth.

Nasal Breathing

This is a very easy exercise to start with. It should be second nature to everyone in the room but the idea is to think about your breathing.

1. Breathe out slowly through your nose to empty your lungs (for a count of three). As your lungs empty your stomach muscles will tighten and your belly will flatten slightly.

2. Now relax the stomach muscles and breathe in fresh, clean air through the nose (for a count of two). Allowing the breath to sink naturally into your body, place your hands just below your belly button and feel your stomach swell.

3. Once your stomach feels full of air, empty your lungs once again by breathing out through the nose as before.

Repeat the process for several minutes; don't force the breath; be mindful and calm.

Please take care if you (or anyone doing this technique) have difficulties with breathing (asthma, bronchial problems, etc.). If so, you *must* remember to count to three on the out breath and two on the in. (*If in doubt, please consult your doctor prior to undertaking this training.*)

Chi

Chi, meaning vital energy, is vital for life. It is believed that when the Chi is good then health will be good.

Chi translates as energy or breath. Everything living has Chi (positive and negative). It is not only a physical sensation; stimulating Chi can also result in a physical change, for example, improved circulation. During training we want to cultivate a strong internal attitude and positive Chi.

How to Feel Your Chi

Allow your wrists to go limp and, holding your elbows at shoulder height, shake your hands hard from side to side. Continue this for a count of 20. Now turn your palms out and you should feel them tingle, or perhaps your fingers feel like sausages? Because of the improved circulation of energy/Chi, fingers, arms and/or toes can have a nice feeling, almost as if they are inflated or swollen. Some people also report warmth or tingles in the hands and arms when stimulating Chi. This movement of energy is the feeling of Chi.

Or, you could squeeze and release a fist repeatedly and hard with just one hand. When you stop, your hand will tingle and if you then hold both palms in front of you, palm up, and relax, you can transfer that feeling from one to the other – magic!

Shake Off Negativity

Tutorial 1 @ 00.22

Shake off negativity

During Tai Chi/Qigong practice we want to let go of tension, gripping or holding on. You could try one (or both) of the following techniques:

1.   Lift one foot, shake it vigorously and then repeat with the other. You can hold onto a wall or the back of a chair for balance.

2.   Or, shake the whole body to release any tension. This is fun.

When a dog (or animal) walks on all fours, its organs hang from the spine. Because humans now walk upright our organs do not hang freely and can often become tight and tense. To give the internal organs a light massage – shake the body!

Chi Brushing

Once our Chi is flowing freely through our bodies we need to ensure that any bad, stale or negative Chi is banished and replaced with good, positive Chi. This is done by brushing away the old Chi and encouraging new Chi or energy to flow into the area.

This exercise can be done alone or in pairs. However, please ensure that participants are happy with this hands-on technique.

During Tai Chi we want to encourage you to forget about the past (fear, problems, pressure from outside sources).

According to Chinese medicine fear blocks learning and could lead to learning problems.

Chi Brushing Yourself

1. Allow the left arm to hang down by your side in a relaxed manner.

2. With your right hand, brush firmly down the outside of the left arm and as you reach the end of the fingers pull off the old Chi and throw it onto the floor. (Do not throw it onto someone else as this is a bit like giving your horrible old cold to your friend – not very nice at all!)

3. Brush in a long sweep all the way down the outside of your left leg.

4. Brush the top of your foot and sweep all the old Chi onto the floor.

Now the other side.

Chi Brushing with a Partner

Please ensure that your partner is happy with the following hands-on exercise. Ask if it's OK before you start and always Treat your partner with respect.

1. Stand behind your partner as they relax with their hands hanging down by their sides.

2. Take the palm of your left hand and place it on your partner's left shoulder – this is to ground yourself.

3. With the palm of your right hand brush across the shoulders left to right (as if you are brushing something off).

4. Keeping your hand on your partner's shoulder, brush down the *outside* of their arm, over the hand and gently pull the old Chi from the tips of their fingers and throw it on the floor.

5. Run the palm of your right hand down the *outside* of their leg while still keeping your left hand on their shoulder. (Never impose yourself on your partner as this can be intimidating.)

6. Brush the old Chi from their foot and onto the floor. (The hands on the shoulder can swap over to allow you to brush each leg, one at a time – it is quite tricky but you will be able to work it out easily enough.)

Repeat down the other side.

Swap places with your partner and repeat the exercise.

Flexibility

In China it is considered very important to maintain good health for as long as possible.

In Western society we don't think much about our health until we experience a problem. For example, falls account for a large amount of accidents (in some instances fatalities) in the elderly population. Some of these incidents can be put down to reduced flexibility. Our flexibility is impaired as we grow older which can lead to joint instability and falls.

We could maintain our flexibility by practising Tai Chi and/or Qigong on a regular basis. It is very important for us to maintain flexibility from a young age.

If Tai Chi were a plant, it would be bamboo: extremely strong but also incredibly flexible. Practising Tai Chi or Qigong on a daily basis will help you stay flexible and supple.

Figure of Eight on its Side

Tutorial 1 @ 01.08

To get the most out of Tai Chi you will learn in time that the body (torso) moves the arms.

Try this:

1. With your right arm draw a figure of eight on its side in the air.

2. Try again, and this time make your arm move by turning your body and allowing your 'trunk' or 'torso' to move your arm. The strength comes from your 'root'.

Repeat several times.

Tai Chi classics say the energy comes up from the ground, is rooted in the feet and turned at the waist. It then travels up the back over the shoulders and is expressed in the hands.

Turn Body and Flop Arms

Turn body & flop arms

You could use this instead of Shaking or the Figure of Eight.

1. Stand in a wide Tai Chi/Qigong Ready Stance position (see pages 43–44).

2. Take your arms out to the side.

3. Make your arms flop round your body by turning your torso to move your arms.

4. Keep your feet firmly on the floor because the strength comes from your root.

5. Turn from the torso and allow your arms to flop round your body. Flop the back of the left hand firmly but gently onto the kidney region on the right of the spine, and flop the right hand onto the spleen (just under the ribs on your left-hand side). As you turn and flop, the hand that pats the back of the body is always palm out. The hand that pats the front of the body is always palm in.

Keep turning and flopping.

6. Now take the arms a little higher and allow the flop to work its way up the body, gently patting the spine at the back of your neck with your hands (don't overstretch).

Keep turning and flopping.

7. Now flop the hands onto the front of the shoulders (between the arm and the chest there is a little hollow called the Shoulder's Nest) – pat gently.

Come slowly to a halt and feel all the energy coursing through your body.

CHI FOR CHILDREN

THE BASICS

Sequence of Training

Five Element Qigong Exercises

Stances

Sounds

Fire Qigong

Earth Qigong

Metal Qigong

Water Qigong

Wood Qigong

Managing the Mind

Building the Bridge

Tai Chi Form: Postures

Counting

Playing with the Dragon in the Clouds

Snake Creeps Down

Golden Cockerel Stands on One Leg

Closing and Some Fun

Polishing Palms

Five Element Qigong Exercises

Stances

There are several stances used in Tai Chi and Qigong and by learning to do them correctly you and your students will receive greater benefit from the exercises you undertake.

READY STANCE IN QIGONG

1. Stand with your feet directly under your hips and your hips directly under your shoulders with feet parallel. This is a guideline so you need to judge a comfortable distance for you (and each student must judge their own).

2. Imagine that you are suspended by a *silver thread* from the top of your head to the clouds and allow a feeling of weightlessness to take over your body. This technique allows the chin to drop slightly in a relaxed manner and elongates the neck, bringing the head and spine into alignment.

3. When you turn from the body (or torso) you should be able to do so from a central axis (like the centre of a wheel), keeping the shoulders level and dropping any tension from them.

READY STANCE IN TAI CHI

Ready Stance for Tai Chi is slightly different to Qigong. For Tai Chi the stance is wider and the palms of your hands must be facing the floor.

HORSE STANCE IN TAI CHI AND SINGLE WHIP

1. This is twice the width of Ready Stance. First, take a step out with either the left or right foot, keeping the feet parallel.

2. Turn the toes out slightly (at a 45 degree angle), bend the knees slightly and relax into a comfortable position. The weight should be dropped down to the feet and distributed evenly between them. Sit as if sitting on a horse.

3. Relax the pelvis and allow your 'tail' (the tailbone at the bottom of the spine) to point to the floor.

4. To change Horse Stance into Single Whip simply raise the right arm and form a beak-like shape with the fingers of the right hand (see Single Whip on page 110).

VIP

The knees must not extend beyond the toes or fall in or out. When you look down, the crease of your trousers should fall onto the bridge of the foot – the strongest point.

FORWARD STANCE IN TAI CHI

Tutorial 2 @ 06.35

When moving forward or back we adopt traditional Wudang Sloping Stance (also known as Forward Stance). You are aiming to have the whole body sloping forward from the back foot to the top of the head at a 45 degree angle with 90 per cent of your weight on the front (or back) foot.

Forward Stance uses the 'core' to support the back – and will develop a nice strong abdominal region or 'six pack'.

Sounds

The Five Element Qigong exercises are accompanied by sounds. These should be mindful and like a 'rumble' projected from deep within the body cavity, to help dispel stagnant Chi.

You can experience this rumble by placing your hand on your ribs and producing a deep 'belly laugh' to *feel* the movement of the air being expelled.

Caution must be taken by practitioners who have bronchial problems.

In China healthcare is considered a preventative measure. Qigong exercises are practised every day, to develop and maintain good health.

Practice usually takes place early in the morning under trees to benefit from the best air quality.

The aim is to live a long, healthy and *youthful* life.

In general in the West we don't think about our health until we have a chronic problem, which then takes longer to heal.

We service our cars regularly but not our bodies!

Fire Qigong

This is an exercise for the heart.

The fire element relates to impatience. This Qigong can help reduce impatience and cultivate positive energy (joy).

This exercise improves circulation throughout the body. The heart is our body's ruler, like an emperor, and by looking after this essential organ other organs will also benefit.

Tutorial 1 @ 02.17

This exercise will cause you (and your students) to laugh, which is the aim of this Qigong, but don't tell them this in advance. However, tell your students that they will experience an emotion (your students could research 'emotions'). Whatever this emotion is, just let it go – nothing is wrong.

If you have high blood pressure *do not* undertake this exercise without prior agreement by your doctor.

Try this exercise first thing in the morning, especially if you're feeling down. Keep going for at least ten minutes. Even if you don't start laughing, anyone within hearing distance will!

Stand in Ready Stance keeping the knee and elbow joints soft, with the weight evenly distributed between the feet, which are rooted to the ground (don't swing your weight from foot to foot). You may wish to experiment with your stance to find a width that is comfortable for you.

1. Raise the right arm from the shoulder, arm and hand stretched out at forehead height, palm turned out. Bend (or drop) the elbow (keeping the arm horizontal). Bring the left hand across the front of the body, palm out, and point the fingers up to the right hand. This now looks like a window.

2. Look through the window and push out to the right, as if pushing something away from you. Keep the feet firmly on the ground.

3. Keeping the feet firmly rooted, turn from the torso to face the left. Reverse the movements so that the left arm is raised to shoulder height and the right hand points up to the left hand.

As you push make a *low* rumbling sound, 'Haaaa' from the lungs, allowing the sound to vibrate throughout the body to expel old Chi. (Don't shout but allow the breath to come from way inside). Repeat on the left and continue as a sequence.

This exercise generates a lot of laughter so encourage your students to have fun with it. When exhaling, you could encourage your students to imagine the 'Haaaa' is similar to breathing onto a window!

Earth Qigong

This is an exercise for the spleen called the Yellow Emperor.

The earth element relates to worry. This Qigong can help reduce worry and cultivate positive energy (sympathy). The spleen is damaged by overthinking or worry. For example, when students 'cram' for exams, they can induce what Chinese medicine considers spleen-related disorders such as weakened immunity and a tendency towards coughs and colds. This exercise (as it is directly related to the spleen) can help alleviate these symptoms.

This is a good Qigong to do before and during winter to boost the immune system.

An ancient story tells about the long, good health of the Yellow Emperor, who was known for bringing peace and prosperity to his region of China. He lived for 100 years. When asked what the secret behind his long, good health was, he said that it was because he practised Spleen Brushing 100 times *every* day – for 100 years!

Tutorial 1 @ 03.07

1. Start this exercise in Ready Stance.

2. Place your right palm on the side of your left ribs.

3. Pull your right palm across the front of the body to the right hand side of the abdomen.

4. Place your left palm over your left ribs, pushing it across to the right and following with the right hand in a smoothing motion. Repeat as often as possible (maximum 100) and allow the heat in the hands to penetrate. Finish by reversing the pull towards the left (five times), resting the palms at the end over the left side of the ribs (on the Spleen).

Metal Qigong

This is an exercise for the lungs.

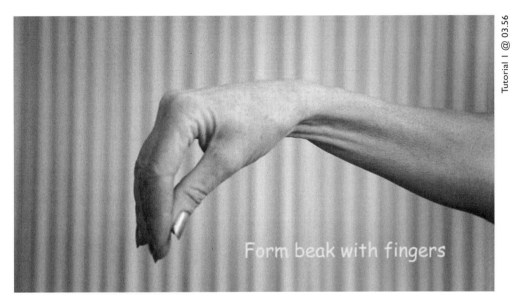

Form beak with fingers

Tutorial I @ 03.56

Breathing is a big part of this exercise, so encourage children to really 'go for it' when making the noise as it will help them make full use of their lungs, cleansing them completely. Please also read important information on breathing (see VIP on page 118).

1. Start this exercise in Ready Stance.

2. Stretch out both arms so you make a T shape at shoulder height, fingers touching at the thumb and forefinger and middle finger (to form a beak).

The metal element relates to grief. This Qigong can help banish negative energy (sorrow) and allow positive energy (courage) to develop. Guide the mind to a feeling of 'letting go'.

Metal Qigong

Tutorial I @ 04.19

3.   Bring your arms slowly to the front, retaining their height, and as you breathe out make the sound of a snake: 'Sssssssss' (imagine steam cleaning the lungs). When exhaling imagine the steam being white in colour to help cleanse the mind.

4.   Breathe in as you pull the arms back out to the sides and open the chest. Repeat as a sequence. Use your core structure/abdominal muscles to hold your arms up. This is surprisingly *hard work* – don't repeat more than is comfortable but do put in some effort.

Do *not* do this exercise if you are pregnant or have high blood pressure.

Water Qigong

This an exercise for the kidneys.

The water element relates to fear. This Qigong can help reduce fear and cultivate positive energy (gentleness/compassion). According to Chinese medicine, fear is stored in the kidneys and can block learning. In fact, scientific research recognizes that fear and stress can weaken memory and create learning difficulties.[6]

A good technique to reduce fear is to heat the kidney area. You could do this by giving the kidney region in your back a good hard rub and/or have a nice warm bath.

The following exercise is particularly good for relieving these symptoms because it's energetic. As you bend over towards the feet you are pumping energy from the Bubbling Well (located near the ball of the foot) up the back of the legs to the kidneys. The legs should be straight *but not* locked. The purpose is to feel a strong stretch up the back of the legs – remember to stay within your limitations. You will be able to touch your toes in time! It is also good for posture and spine alignment and for strengthening the lower back.

---

6   Conner, M. (2007) 'We Have Nothing to Fear but Fear of Learning.' Available at www.fastcompany.com/resources/learning/conner/011607.html, accessed 8 April 2011.

Tutorial I @ 05.54

1. Start this exercise in Ready Stance.

2. Place the back of your right hand, palm out, in front of your forehead and the left hand, palm out, on the kidney on your lower back at the right-hand side of your spine.

3. Stretch open the fleshy part between your thumb and finger (called the Tiger's Mouth), resting the thumb on the spine with the hand facing palm out.

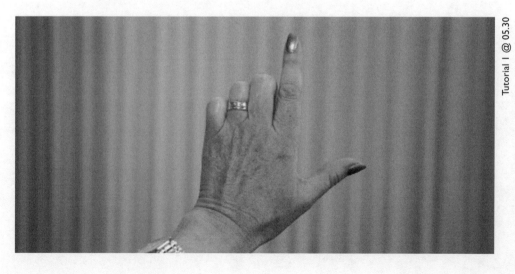

Tutorial I @ 05.30

'Tiger's Mouth' – the soft fleshy part between the thumb and forefinger.

4. Keeping the legs straight but *not locked*, bend over slowly and scoop the hand (palm upwards) turning the body in a clockwise direction and bending over as low as is comfortable. Turn the hand palm out as you stand up and palm down as you bend over, as if to scoop up water. It is also like drawing a circle in the air from above your forehead to the ground and back.

As you begin to scoop, breathe out making the noise, 'Foooo', like a low rumble.

You *should* feel a stretch in the pelvic area and down the back of the legs.

Take care to stay within your own limitations.

Repeat on the other side and then as a sequence. Remember to breathe out gently as you bend over and breathe in on the way up.

You can guide your students to engage their imagination by suggesting that they are standing in a beautiful, warm, clear pool of water. As they bend over they scoop a handful of this beautiful, energizing water and as they stand up they imagine the warm water running down the arm, over the shoulder and into the Tiger's Mouth which is resting on the kidney point. They are therefore giving a little TLC (tender loving care) to these organs.

Wood Qigong

This is an exercise for the liver.

The wood element relates to the liver (located beneath the right-hand side of your ribs). According to TCM the liver is the organ that relates to anger, frustration and other negative emotions. These emotions may be linked to fear or anxiety. This exercise helps us expel the negative emotions while allowing positive energy (kindness) to develop.

It has been found that Tai Chi can be helpful for some students with ADHD (attention deficit hyperactivity disorder). This Qigong may help initially to bring short-term improvements. With continued practice attention levels may be extended.

Tutorial I @ 07.42

1. Start this exercise in Ready Stance.

2. Curl your hands into a light fist (as though holding a baby bird) and rest your forearms on your hips, relaxing the shoulders.

3. Push one hand forward, and turn the fist to push hand palm forward, as if pushing something away from you. Extend the arm in front of you with the other tucked in an upturned fist at your waist.

4. Slowly swap positions, pulling the extended arm in and pushing the other out. Coordinate the palm change as the hands pass each other in a smooth movement.

As you bring the palms together, imagine you are polishing a large emerald to make it shine, or turning on a laser beam that is radiating from the palm of one hand to the other. Perhaps you can hear the laser beam? This movement will become natural very quickly.

5. As you push, breathe out and make the steam train noise, 'Shhoooo'.

6. Feel the waist turning as you push and pull. Keep going.

A good way of getting children into the spirit of this exercise is to tell them they are making a noise like a steam train. They know instantly what you mean and it adds to the fun. You can do this exercise facing a friend or partner in a 'push me/pull me' motion.

Managing the Mind

As we go into our Tai Chi training we want to encourage a more internal focus. Practising the following techniques during training will help you achieve this.

THE MANIC MONKEY

The Chinese call the mind the Manic Monkey. I'm sure you know why. The Manic Monkey will command our thoughts 24/7 and pull us every which way!

To control the Manic Monkey practise the following technique.

Building the Bridge

This technique is also called Tip of the Tongue to Roof of the Mouth.

In TCM it is recognized that there are two main energy channels located on the front and back of the body. The front channel is called the Conception Vessel, containing the Yin circulation (more about Yin and Yang to follow). This vessel starts from the lower lip and extends down the front at the centre of the body to the perineum or Sea Bottom.

The vessel on the back is called the Governing Vessel and contains the Yang circulation. It starts from the Sea Bottom outside the spine, passing up the back and over the top of the head and ends at the roof of the mouth. These two vessels are not connected until you Build the Bridge.

If you teach only one thing, make it Building the Bridge.

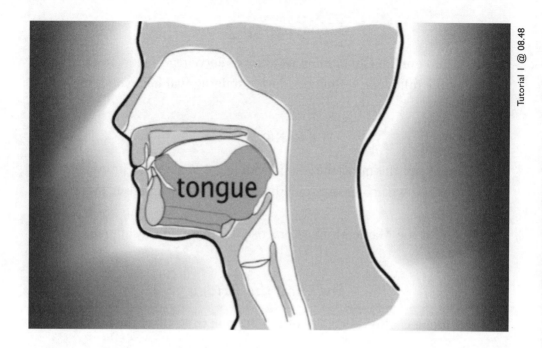

Touch the tip of your tongue to the roof of your mouth, just behind the top teeth (run your tongue along the roof of your mouth until you come across a little indentation). Gently press the tip of the tongue into the indentation and relax the jaw and teeth. Breathe in and out through the nose allowing the breath to drop to the abdomen slowly.

By doing this the Yin/Yang vessels are connected and the circuit is complete allowing the Chi to circulate around the body. This tongue touch is called Da Qiao (Building the Bridge), a technique which will drop you into a state of meditation, calm and relaxation.

Use this technique for any stressful event such as exams, interviews, presentations.

Do not Build the Bridge when driving.

Tai Chi Form: Postures

Tai Chi is an exercise that relies on the union of mind and body. Children are not self-aware enough to understand how their focus and concentration also help their physical and emotional wellbeing and vice versa. However, they can learn how to appreciate this by training in Tai Chi.

It is the slow, mindful way in which Tai Chi is performed that brings about this union and a child of five can reap the same rewards as an adult by taking part in the same exercise.

Regular training can help children understand that their emotions can be just short-lived and that they can draw on their ability to return to calmness. Feeling continually in the grip of emotions can be a major cause of ill health in the future.[7] With this understanding we can learn how to manage feelings and control our responses to the emotions.

The essence of Tai Chi movement is to be totally *in the moment*; not thinking about the last move or the next, but concentrating purely on where you are here and now. When you consider that it derives from a martial art this makes perfect sense.

Counting

When practising the Tai Chi postures, it is useful to count out the movements as an aid to learning and also to keep everyone in time and moving together. It is especially useful when teaching large groups. We do not count the movements in Qigong.

The reason we count in Cantonese is that this was the dialect of the working class people, spoken in Southern China and Hong Kong where Wudang Tai Chi was widely taught. Mandarin was the language of the upper classes and scholars. Mandarin is now the more predominant dialect in China but we retain the history of Wudang Tai Chi by counting in Cantonese.

---

7   Source: Little Yin Chinese Therapies (www.littleyin.co.uk).

We are going to count some of the movements in Cantonese, a dialect used mainly in Southern China. You will be counting Yat where you see 1, Yee where you see 2 and San where you see 3.

> 1 = Yat
>
> 2 = Yee
>
> 3 = San

Playing with the Dragon in the Clouds

This is a calming exercise that is practised in smooth wave-like movements. It is designed to promote rhythmical breathing and relaxation.

Playing with the dragon in the clouds

Tutorial 1 @ 09.27

Start this exercise in Horse Stance or from Single Whip (see Tutorial 3).

Playing with the dragon in the clouds

1. Hold your arms up in front of you with your hands, palms out, at shoulder height. (Note: if your hands were to drop they would land on your lap.)

2. Turn the torso to the right (upper body) and drop your left hand in front of your tummy (palm in), then bring it round in front of the body, until it meets and is in front of your right hand (which has remained where it started). You should now have your left hand in front of your right hand, as if holding a ball. At this point imagine you have a dragon between your hands and you are holding its tail.

3. From this position bring the right hand down in a similar swoop and slowly turn from the torso to bring the left hand, palm out, back across at chin level, right hand, palm in, at tummy level.

    The hands will face each other, as if holding a ball on the left-hand side of the body. At this point imagine you are holding the dragon's head.

Keep going, concentrating on the movement, and we will now add mindful techniques to this posture to enhance the outcome.

As you repeat this movement, breathe in and out through the nose, allowing the breath to fall and the abdomen to expand, as in the warm-up exercise (see page 32).

For the younger age group engage the mind by using the imagination. Guide the student to paint a story by asking questions about their dragon.

For example, imagine that there is a dragon in front of you and as you put your palms out the dragon comes across to play. His or her head is in one hand and tail in the other. Let's start to stroke our dragon to help it feel happier/ calmer/fearless (tell me how your dragon feels).

Everyone's dragon is different. In our hands we have a magic Chi paintbrush and, as we stroke our dragon, we are going to paint it a special colour.

CALMING TECHNIQUES

The teacher can now lead the students through the calming techniques by pausing for the moment and asking them to add on the following techniques:

- Lightly breathe in and out through the nose.
- Feel the tummy expand with the breath.
- Build the Bridge (place tip of tongue to roof of mouth).
- Now try to look towards the tip of the nose.
- Breathe in.
- Breathe out.

Encourage your students by gently repeating the above.

Ask your students to imagine their own special dragon. Ask questions (some suggestions follow) while continuing to Play with the Dragon in the Clouds.

- How does it feel as you run your hand from the dragon's head to the dragons' tail?

- What colour is your dragon? For example, the following colours relate to emotions/physical sensations:

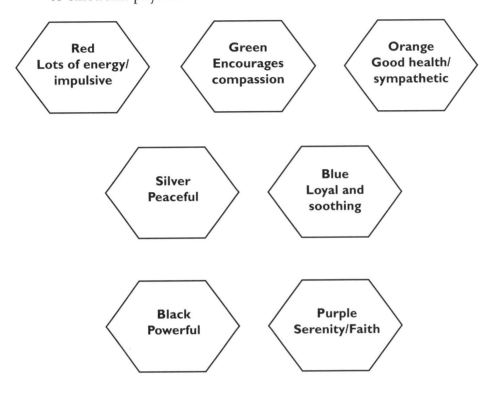

- How does he/she feel?

- What's your dragon's name? My dragon is called Wu!

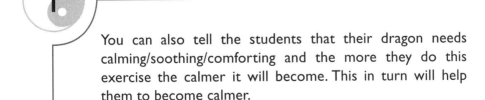

You can also tell the students that their dragon needs calming/soothing/comforting and the more they do this exercise the calmer it will become. This in turn will help them to become calmer.

From experience, Playing with the Dragon in the Clouds is the exercise that most kids want to do. They also remember it well and can help others to learn. They can do this with a partner and learn about 'mirror image', also improving their skills in timing and cooperation with another person.

As a teacher this is really exciting to watch, because you see children problem solving.

A group of kids will really concentrate on this exercise and often teachers/parents point excitedly at them being quiet, calm and in 'the zone'.

Snake Creeps Down

Tutorial 1 @ 10.24

It is easier to teach this posture with your back to your students. To make sure everyone is moving at the same time, count the movements. *Reminder:* you will be counting Yat where you see 1, Yee where you see 2 and San where you see 3.

This is a difficult exercise, deliberately put into the programme as a challenge. It can follow in a sequence from Playing with the Dragon in the Clouds. The postures in this exercise help improve core structure and flexibility.

Please follow healthy guidelines and ensure that your students are not bending over during this exercise but sinking to the floor. The Qigong exercise Planting Feet on the Ground (Tutorial 2) can also help improve core strength.

1. From Playing with the Dragon in the Clouds, hold your arms up in front of you with your hands, palms out, at shoulder height.

2. Move your weight onto the right foot and turn your left foot out to your left.

3. Point the left arm so that it follows the line of the left foot.

1. Take the weight back onto the left foot.

2. In a small circling motion bring the right hand over and point to the left, taking the left hand to the inside of the right elbow crease.

At the same time, *gently* swivel your right heel out and place it on the floor. Now point your right toe out and place it on the floor (to lengthen the stance).

3. In a small circling motion change the hands over once more, pointing with the left hand, right hand to the inside of the left elbow crease. (This is almost like your arms are doing the pedalling on a bike).

1. Point the left hand to the left toe (or knee) *keeping your back straight*. Pull both arms up the left leg as if pulling a big snake out of the grass. Begin to transfer some weight onto the right foot and sink a little.

2. Throw the snake into the air, pointing the left hand to the roof and the right hand facing the elbow crease (very specific), and look at your hands.

3. Turn your torso to the right bringing your arms around in a circle in front of you (like the hands on a clock). As your hands reach 4 o'clock, sink down a little, taking 95 per cent of the weight onto the right foot and off of the left foot.

1. Turn your torso until both hands are pointing to the left and swivel on the empty left foot until it is facing forwards.

2. Stand up by lifting your right foot and placing it under your right hip (the right foot will be behind the left foot rather than level with it) with your feet facing forwards.

3. You are now in a Forward Stance with your weight on the left leg, your upper body sloping forward – keeping the back straight. You are facing to the left, body square on, with your feet facing forwards.

Finish with the left hand above the forehead, palm facing out and up (to protect the head) and the right hand, palm down, below the waist (to protect the Kwa – Chinese for groin!).

It's a good idea to practise each movement independently until you or your students are really confident with it.

It is *very* important that you or your students do not lean forward as you turn as this would put too much pressure on the lower back. We also want to encourage a stretch up the inside of the legs so it is important that you should start in Horse Stance. This should not be too wide, otherwise you could do the splits and pull a hamstring. Remember, this move can follow straight on from the previous one or be practised in isolation. It is an excellent test of balance and focus.

I encourage students to imagine a big snake and lead them through the actions with a story (see below). Alternatively, you could make up your own relevant story.

To improve this posture, practise the Qigong Planting Feet on the Ground (Tutorial 2) as your practice deepens.

ENGAGE YOUR STUDENTS' IMAGINATION

As you start the posture say:

'Point your left hand out towards the snake (at the wall/door).

Reach out to pull him in.

He slithered away, so try again – point the right hand.

Missed – try again with the left.

The snake is now under your left foot, so you are going to bend over and pull it out.

Pull the snake straight up your leg and throw it in the air.

Point your left hand forward high above your head and right hand in at the elbow crease.

Keep your eyes on the snake as it curls its big body in front of you!

Catch the snake, turn the body and push him out of the room/door.

Stand up and Guard against him coming back – this posture is hard work!'

Hold the final posture in Snake Creeps Down for a second or two and then settle into Guard Position.

GUARD POSITION

Finish with the left hand above the forehead, palm facing out and up (to protect the head) and the right hand, palm down, below the waist (to protect the Kwa – Chinese for groin!).

Your left foot is in a Forward Stance with your weight on the left leg, your upper body slightly angled forward, utilizing the core for stability. Keep the back straight.

You are now facing forward, body square on, with your feet facing forwards.

Golden Cockerel Stands on One Leg

Golden Cockerel stands on one leg

Tutorial 1 @ 11.00

1. From the final posture, Guard, you will have the left foot in front of the right with your arms out in front of you.

2. Retain your balance on your left foot and imagine that you are rooted like a big tree – all the way to China.

3. Raise your right hand and as if it is attached to the right foot by a piece of string, gently lift the right foot off the ground until the knee is directly in front of you. Right foot and hand move together.

If possible, turn the sole of the right foot slightly inwards towards your left knee. At the same time raise your right hand to eye level.

Breathe in slowly through your nose, count to five and exhale. Or stand proud and tall for as long as you feel comfortable – this will get better in time!

Lower your right leg. If this was easy you could repeat the move with the left foot. In fact, try this now.

Tutorial 1 @ 11.08

Ask your students if they know what a cockerel is. A good point of reference for them is the film *Chicken Run* and the character Rocky.

VIP

Improving external balance helps the internal balance and calms the mind. Younger students find this difficult at first, but keep practising and it will improve – they will be really pleased when they succeed at this exercise.

AN ANCIENT CHINESE STORY

An ancient Tai Chi master constantly advised her students to 'relax through the feet into the ground'. 'We should not be standing on our own two feet but standing on the ground', creating a feeling of balance, support and comfort. 'A person who is standing relaxed and sunk feels as stable as Mount Tai.'

Remember to feel as though you are connected to the clouds from a silver thread from the top of the head in order to support you and help your balance. This suspended feeling is called Li Shou (empty top and heavy bottom or base).

Closing and Some Fun

It is now the end of the lesson and you should always close down. This is a physical exercise and a psychological acknowledgement of the work that we have done to cultivate and embrace positive Chi.

Remember how we brushed *off* the old Chi? Now we are going to do a similar thing, only this time in a closing exercise:

1. Place your right hand onto your left shoulder.

2. Brush down the outside of your left arm from the shoulder to the finger tips. Now run your right hand *up* the inside of the left arm.

3. Place your left hand onto the right shoulder and brush down the outside of the right arm and up the inside.

4. Take both hands, palm in, under your armpits, and bending gently, run your hands down the *outside* of your legs.

5. Now run your hands round the outside of the foot and rest them on the ankle bones at the *inside* of the ankles.

6.   *Slowly* stand up straight, running the hands up the inside of your legs (avoiding the groin area) and rest your hands on the Dantien (just under the tummy button).

Close your eyes and breathe in through the nose, dropping the breath and thoughts down to your hands. This is called Grounding your Energy. Gently and slowly open your eyes and bring yourself back into the room.

Every time we practise Tai Chi and Qigong we finish by dropping our thoughts to the Dantien.

Polishing Palms

The following exercises form part of an ancient system practised to cultivate (or feel) Chi. Ask your students to choose a friend or partner that they are comfortable working with.

1.   Stand facing your partner. Ask your partner to hold out his or her left hand, palm up.

2.   Place your right hand a few inches above their hand at the Laogong point (palm of the hands) and imagine a bright red laser beam pointing from your hand to theirs: do *not* touch hands. This is similar to the technique where we activated the laser beam in the Wood Qigong.

3.   Now as your partner's hand remains still, slowly circle your right hand in small anticlockwise circles, as though the centre of your hands are connected.

Do *not* touch your partner.

4. Continue to draw a circle in your imagination onto your friend's hand.

5. Begin to increase the circumference of the circle and imagine the laser beam getting stronger.

6. Increase the circle taking in the fingers – do you feel anything?

After several circles change direction (circle your hand in a clockwise direction).

Now reflect on the exercise:

- Do you and your friend feel any difference?

- What sensation is produced by making the circles?

- And what sensation is produced when you extend the circle?

Perhaps you can feel a warm feeling (Yang) or was the sensation cold (Yin)? With time and concentration you can extend the feeling of Chi up your partner's arm.

This exercise will help you wind down and could help you to sleep better.

Tutorial

2

CHI FOR CHILDREN
CENTRING AND BALANCING

Sequence of Training

Qigong Exercises

Slowing an Excited Heart with Qigong Breathing

Holding up the Sky with the Arms

Yin/Yang Hands

Planting the Feet on the Ground

Pulling the Bow to Shoot the Arrow

Tai Chi Form: Postures

Step Back and Push the Monkey

Holding the Golden Plate

Curtsey to the Queen

Spreading the Wings (or Close Form)

About this Programme

This programme has been specifically designed with techniques to centre the mind and body.

As we know, techniques from the ancient Chinese arts of Tai Chi and Qigong can help induce a state of calmness. Within this state we are then more able to manage our anxieties, settle nerves and so feel reassured and more in control.

These techniques are particularly useful when we are under pressure, for example, before exams, interviews, presentations and more.

The calming exercises have been chosen because they help to engage both hemispheres of the brain. Referred to as cross-lateral thinking, this creates internal balance.

In vertical or linear thinking we utilize the logical or mathematical side of the brain but learning how to interconnect both sides of the brain gives us the lateral thinking which is connected with new ideas (i.e. entrepreneurial thinking or thinking outside the box!).

Scientists have discovered that when rats were taught new motor skills the neurons in the motor cortex of their brains increased. Similarly, we believe that the human brain can benefit from learning a sequence of movements.

You will learn how to open meridians and feel the movement of Chi which will help to generate calm energy.

More about Qigong

From experience we recognize that practising Qigong will move any stagnant (or blocked) Chi in the meridians and improve the flow of energy throughout the body. However, we may not sense this immediately because of stagnation.

At a physical level stagnation could feel like an ache or a pain in the muscles or joints. However, it is important for us to recognize that stagnation also affects our mental function. The stagnation of Chi in the mind is just as harmful as blocked Chi in the body. Stagnation can also result in black moods or a feeling of 'not moving forward'.

For both adults and children, a black mood is a very bad place to be and it is helped enormously by physical movement. During Tai Chi and Qigong practice, we aim to remove this stagnation. It's simply a case of moving the Chi!

The aim of this tutorial is to 'manage the mind'.

Qigong Exercises

Slowing an Excited Heart with Qigong Breathing

In this exercise we will be concentrating on the lower Dantien which is situated two-fingers width below the tummy button and is considered to be the centre of gravity and a storage area for energy.

You can practise this exercise standing, sitting or lying down. The technique adopts Nasal Breathing, so if you suffer from nasal congestion you can breathe through the mouth.

To remind you: your mental state has a profound effect on your breathing. When we are distressed or angry, breathing becomes shallower and faster and the heartbeat quickens. This can result in hyperventilation, which is not desirable.

The ideal way is to breathe slowly and deeply, using the diaphragm muscle and abdomen/tummy. As practice develops you can monitor the changes. The average person takes approximately 10 to 16 breaths per minute. After practising Qigong for some time, this can be reduced to five or less!

Don't force the breath, but listen internally, and develop these techniques over time.

Try this now: you should begin to feel the abdomen rising and falling with the breath and this is not just caused by the inflation of the lungs, it is where the movement of the Chi in the abdomen is stimulated by the breath. Concentrate on this feeling – the Yi (mind) leads the Chi (energy).

It is important to have the emphasis on the out breath. Everyone finds it easy to take in a big gulp of air. However, the aim is to draw in the breath through the nose gradually, feeling that it is long, smooth and fine, like a ribbon, and letting it drop to the Dantien. You can remember how to breathe more fully with the following four simple instructions:

1. Exhale gently through the nose.

2. At the end of the out breath you should feel the stomach muscles slightly tighten and your tummy flatten slightly. You have now dispelled all of the stale air in the lungs and allowed room for clean air to replace it.

We cannot live without this process taking place, but often breathing is shallow and high in the chest. This is a classic sign of tension or anxiety and can lead to health problems.

3. Relax the stomach muscles, breathe in through the nose and allow the breath to sink naturally. The tummy should swell like a balloon. Again don't force this, or you will create tension.

4. Once your tummy feels full of air, exhale again.

A good way to keep the mind quiet in this exercise is to count the breath:

- As you breathe out and empty the mind see a big black number **1** in your mind's eye.

- As you breathe in count **2**.

- Breathe out **3**.

- Breathe in **4**.

- And so on…

When your mind wanders, you have to start the count at 1 again!

Holding up the Sky with the Arms

Tutorial 2 @ 01.00

These are strengthening exercises from the Yi Jin Jing Qigong programme, part of physical exercises practised in China for postural alignment and conditioning.

Stand with the feet shoulder distance apart, feet pointing forwards (to make this more stable you could widen the stance slightly).

1. Raise the hands slowly out to the side with palms facing up.

2. Stretch them up over your head, palms still facing up. Ensure that fingers are pointing inwards and just touching as if you are holding up the sky!

3. At the same time lift your heels slightly off the ground and touch the tongue to the roof of the mouth (Building the Bridge). Engage the core by gently drawing the Dantien (below your tummy button) towards your spine. Inhale deeply, concentrating on your hands.

4. Make the hands into fists and lower the arms from over the head to shoulder level (out to the sides). Keep some tension in your arms.

5. At the same time allow the heels to sink to the floor. Bend knees slightly and repeat five to ten times.

Yin/Yang Hands

Tutorial 2 @ 01.55

This is a sinew stretching exercise.

Take care to work within your body's frame – do not overstretch.

1. Cross the hands in front of the chest, palms facing inwards, right hand outside of left.

2. Drop both hands down and out, in a stretch finishing with the right hand palm facing backwards, and the left hand palm facing forwards.

3. Bring the hands back in front of the chest, palms facing inwards, with left hand outside of right hand.

4. Drop both hands down and out, in a stretch finishing with the right hand palm facing forwards, and the left hand palm facing backwards (the opposite of the last time).

This exercise demonstrates Yin and Yang by turning the hands to face in opposite directions. In this example, Yin is backwards and Yang is forwards. Yin and Yang principles are at the heart of Tai Chi and Qigong and you will learn to recognize them in different postures. You will also recognize that rising up is Yang whereas sinking down is Yin. This exercise takes a lot of concentration and encourages relaxation – it's hard to do if you are stiff or trying too hard.

Planting the Feet on the Ground

Tutorial 2 @ 02.56

This exercise improves core stability and strength.

Take a slightly wider stance than in the previous exercise so that your feet are now twice the width of the shoulders. Do not go too wide and ensure that the floor is not slippery, otherwise students could damage muscles. Repeat as is often as comfortable, increasing repetitions as the exercise becomes easier.

1. Bend the knees and take up Horse Stance (see Tutorial 1). Keep the back straight and head erect as if attached to the clouds by a silver thread.

2. With the arms out to the sides, shoulder level, palms down, you should squat slightly and sink, keeping your knees over the bridge of the foot.

3. Fold the arms in front of the chest, with palms of hands facing down.

4. Gently sit down into Horse Stance, keeping the back straight and – if possible – thighs parallel to the floor (similar to a squat).

5. Lower your hands (as if pushing down a ball of Chi). Your hands should finish just above the thighs with fingers pointing towards each other, palms still facing down.

6. Turn palms over and slowly raise them to chest level (as if you were lifting a heavy ball of Chi) and at the same time, rise up from the squat slightly. Relax, sink and finish by crossing arms in front of your body with the right arm outside the left, with the palms of your hands facing your chest. From here go into Pulling the Bow to Shoot the Arrow.

Pulling the Bow to Shoot the Arrow

Tutorial 2 @ 05.56

This is a cross-lateral exercise.

'The foundation for long life is found in the spine. When exercising to stretch the spine, it should be like pulling a bow and shooting the arrow.'[8]

Using this idea to stretch the muscles that support the spine, we are going to imagine that we are pulling a bow. First, we will pull the 'bow' to its utmost length and pause for a second, then let it go as if shooting an arrow.

Keep the back straight.

Start in Horse Stance – relaxed but sunk – with the thighs as close to parallel to the ground as possible.

1. Cross your arms in front of your chest with the right arm outside the left arm. Fingers should be loosely separated. Turn your head and look into the palm of your right hand.

2. Make a light fist with both hands. The right hand is a Tiger's Claw (see image at the top of page 88).

---

8   From the *Internal Classics* and Jade Body Qigong, a translation of which can be found on the website www.qi.org/liu/jadebody.html (under the heading 'The movements').

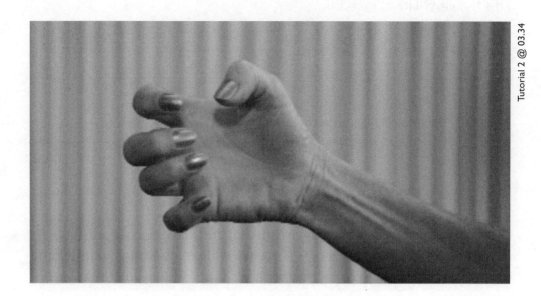

Tutorial 2 @ 03.34

3. Extend both your index finger and thumb of the left hand while keeping the other three fingers curled. Stretch the Tiger's Mouth.

The Tiger's Mouth is the soft fleshy part between the thumb and forefinger (see image below).

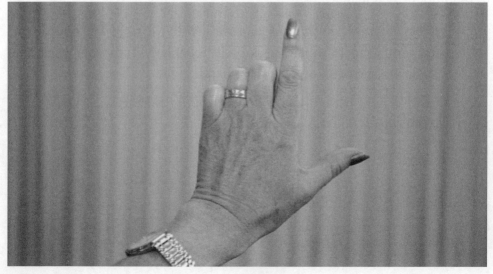

Tutorial 2 @ 03.49

4. Slowly extend the left arm out at shoulder level until it is fully extended. Your eyes should follow the Tiger's Mouth and focus on the fingers.

    At the same time, draw the right hand to the right (as if pulling a bow). Keep the right hand curled in Tiger's Claw. Your right elbow should be pointing out to the right at shoulder level.

5. Open the right hand to 'shoot the arrow'.

> If you or any of your students suffer from heart-related health problems, please ensure that the arms do *not* go higher than heart level.

6. Relax your left hand and bring it back to the front of your chest and at the same time bring the right hand back to the chest. Cross both arms in front of the body – this time with the left arm outside the right arm.

7. Turn the head to the right and look into the palm of the left hand.

8. Make claws with both hands, stretching the index finger and thumb of the right hand.

Then repeat the exercise above but changing sides.

ENCOURAGE THE IMAGINATION

It is important to engage and hold the attention by using the imagination. Throughout the workbook you will come across examples of lively and familiar images that introduce the exercises.

Here is a poem to help with the previous exercise. Encourage your students to join in as this will lead to greater learning.

Outside hand Tiger's Claw.
Inside hand Tiger's Mouth.
Extend the arm to make the arrow.
Pull the hand to pull the bow.
Point the fingers to shoot the arrow.
Cross arms in front of you – so!
Repeat.

To make the exercise aerobic, step up and out between each repetition.

Tai Chi Form: Postures

Tai Chi

Tutorial 2 @ 06.19

As you finished the previous sequence of Tai Chi Postures (Tutorial 1) on Golden Cockerel Stands on One Leg, continue adding to the form with the following sequence:

1. Place the right foot on the ground and drop the right arm.

2. Ground the right foot and lift the left foot and arm.

From there, move into Step Back and Push the Monkey.

Step Back and Push the Monkey

1. Take the arms to the left as if balancing a monkey on your left knee and hold it with your arms (over the left knee).

2. Step straight back with the left leg, placing the foot down, and feel it grounding your posture.

3. Push straight forward with your left hand (in a relaxed manner) – as if pushing the monkey off your knee!

1. Take the weight onto the back (left) foot and ground by sinking the weight.

2. Turn the torso 45 degrees to the right and take the arms over the right knee, as if balancing a monkey on your right knee.

3. Sweep (or slide) straight back with the right leg, placing the foot down and grounding. Push straight forward (in a relaxed manner) with your right hand – as if pushing the monkey off your knee!

Repeat once more with the left leg to complete the sequence.

This exercise is tricky but over time, balance, coordination and spatial awareness will improve. It's a tough but very worthwhile exercise. You could isolate this exercise and practise walking round the room backwards!

Watch you don't bump into anything or anyone.

Walking backwards is quite a common form of exercise in China.

Holding the Golden Plate

Tutorial 2 @ 06.46

The traditional name for this posture is Flying Oblique. However, a little girl in Saltaire Primary School likened the exercise to presenting a plate to the Queen, hence the name for the following Chi for Children postures.

As you finish Step Back and Push the Monkey, your left arm will be in front of your body, your right foot forward in traditional Wudang Sloping Stance (upper body slightly forward with 95 per cent of your weight on the front foot).

Ensure that the knee is over the bridge of the foot.

1. Turn the left hand palm up and fold the right arm across to the pulse point on the left hand, above the wrist and imagine you are Holding a Golden Plate.

93

This could be a beautiful plate laden with lovely food that you are going to present to the Queen. (Every time I do this posture I seem to imagine that I have cucumber sandwiches for the Queen!)

Curtsey to the Queen

Curtsey to the Queen

Tutorial 2 @ 06.51

This is a very powerful stance that will help to build core stability, flexibility and stamina.

Take great care to teach this posture slowly.

From Holding the Golden Plate:

1. Take the weight onto the back (left) foot.

It is necessary to take the weight from the right foot before moving.

Remember in Tai Chi we count the moves Yat 1, Yee 2, and San 3. Now that the weight is removed from the right foot, you can pivot on the right heel, taking the toes out 90 degrees to the right.

2. Turn the upper body 45 degrees to the right and place the weight back onto the right foot.

3. Keeping the upper body as straight as possible (do not bend forward), bend the left knee and place it behind the right heel. *Do not* put the knee on the floor. This is actually like a curtsey.
    Try to look down to the right.

Keep the hands in Holding the Golden Plate but as the body turns to face the right, the hands and arms will be in front of the body.

Finish this posture in Spreading the Wings.

Spreading the Wings (or Close Form)

1. Take the weight slightly forward (to release the back leg), step through with the left foot, stepping out to twice shoulder width but in line with the right foot.

2. Put the left heel down.

3. Ground onto the left foot.

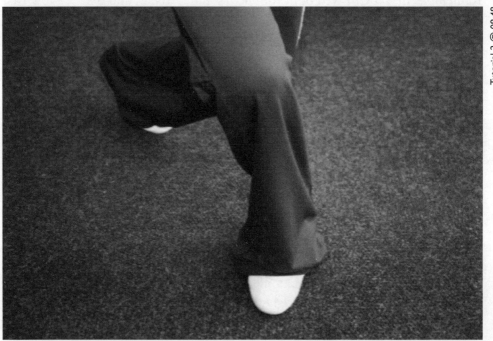

Tutorial 2 @ 08.48

1. Stand up straight. Open the arms in front of the body directly out from each shoulder, like a bird's wings. Turn the left hand palm up and the right hand palm down (if you can).

Tutorial 2 @ 07.15

From here you can sink into Horse Stance and Playing with the Dragon in the Clouds or Close (as in Tutorial 1) to finish.

CLOSE

Congratulations, you have completed Tutorial 2.

3

CHI FOR CHILDREN

OPENING THE FORM

Sequence of Training

Tai Chi Form: Postures

Opening the Form – Inflating the Chi Ball

Ward Off – Holding the Chi Ball

Grasp the Bird's Tail

Single Whip – Forming a Bird's Beak

Closing the Form

About this Programme

Everything in this book has a purpose, and the sequence in which we teach comes from my own experience of teaching the programme to hundreds of students. Tutorial 3 addresses Opening the Form and should be applied to the beginning of the form (see sequence below).

However, let me tell you, although at first it seems simple, it is one of the hardest sequences to teach. By following the step-by-step instructions you will succeed. Take time – be calm.

In Tutorial 3 we refine our Tai Chi Form to help us understand how the body and mind work together.

This module contains more in-depth content and completes the Tai Chi Short Form.

Refinement

As we start to move in Tai Chi, the joints should feel 'open and loose.' This helps towards relaxing and allowing movements to feel more comfortable. In order to allow the joints to be open, imagine a small ball (or egg) nestling in the crease of the elbows, knees and under the arm pits (to allow Chi to flow unhindered).

Do not lock the joints as this causes unnecessary stress. Take *care* if you or your students have a condition called 'hypermobility' or are double jointed, where it is easy to cause damage by overextending.

Tai Chi helps eliminate overextending. This is because we work within a 'frame'. Wudang Tai Chi Chuan comes into the large frame category, that is, if you were to draw a circle from the front foot (in Forward Stance) all the way round to your back heel, no part of the body should extend beyond this circle (do not protrude your bottom, or hands). Keep hips under the posture and head attached by the silver thread to the clouds above.

Relaxation is an ongoing challenge and initially not easy to do. Relaxing and refining the movements work together – just like 'one hand washing the other'.

With prolonged practice, you become deeply aware of your movements and any tension, both in mind and body. Often the tension in the mind is ego driven. Drop the ego and you can find softness. Just acknowledge the area of tension, mental or physical, and continue to practise in a relaxed manner.

Continual practice reduces these tensions.

Coordinate Movement

Coordination is enhanced when we learn Tai Chi.

When a movement is done quickly, as in most sports, there is no recognition of the coordination required. Only when we slow down the movement, as in Tai Chi, do we become aware of balance, for example in shifting the weight from one foot or posture to the other. It is also important to recognize what the hands and feet are doing in relation to one another, and the timing of movements. The body should be coordinated as a whole unit as this is how we unleash the power in Tai Chi. Although the form is done in a slow, relaxed way, there is a definite physical and mental focus required.[9]

---

9   Source: Sifu Ian Cameron, Five Winds School of Tai Chi Chuan, Edinburgh.

Coordinate Mind and Body

Coordination must include the mind *and* the body. As described in Tutorial 2, Tai Chi must be practised in a mindful manner. The mind should be totally immersed in the form. In the Tai Chi classics this is called 'Internalizing the Spirit'. Although there will be distractions, do not allow the mind to get caught up with them – also relate this to your daily activities.

It is impossible to learn Tai Chi quickly and it is the long hours of continual practice that really matter. The truth is that you cannot do the same movement twice. Each time you raise your hands it is a new movement. Practised in this way training is always fresh and creative.[10]

Tai Chi Form: Postures

Opening the Form – Inflating the Chi Ball

Tutorial 3 @ 00.19

---

10   Source: Sifu Ian Cameron.

1. Relax the arms and raise hands to shoulder height as if inflating a great big ball of Chi in front of you. Do not force the movement but maintain a feeling of lightness. Keep the elbows low and relaxed.

2. Draw the arms in towards the Shoulder's Nest by dropping the elbows.

3. Lower the arms to their original position (palms facing the ground).

1. Sink and bend the knees.

Ensure the knees remain above the bridge of the foot.

2. Keeping the weight on the right foot, step forward with the left foot and rest the heel on the ground.

Ward Off – Holding the Chi Ball

Tutorial 3 @ 00.37

1. Circle the left hand in front of the body finishing with the palm facing the chest.

2. Circle the right hand, similar to the left but finishing with the right hand inside the left, as if holding a big Chi ball – fingers of the right hand pointing to the roof.

3. Draw your hands towards you as if attached by a thread. At the same time, draw in the left foot (90 degrees). Shift the weight forward onto the left foot (keep the right foot on the ground).

1. Point the right hand (45 degrees) to the left and look down the arm (to follow the movement).

Tutorial 3 @ 00.46

2. Bend the right knee slightly (which will release the heel from the ground). Having removed weight from the right foot, pivot on the ball of the foot turning the body to the right. Finish facing forwards.

3. Keeping the weight on the left foot step forward, placing the right heel on the ground. At the same time the hands come into Seven Stars posture.

The palm of the right hand faces left. At the same time the fingertips of the left hand are lightly touching the pulse point of the right hand (like Yin and Yang).

The left hand faces in at the wrist.

Keeping the fingers lightly adhered as you turn the hands over Yin becomes Yang and so forth (you could practise this as an exercise on its own).

This completes the opening section of the form up to Seven Stars posture.

Tutorial 3 @ 00.56

Seven Stars posture has a powerful link to Chinese astronomy (not covered in this book), where the star constellation Ursa Major (the Big Dipper) is replicated in the Tai Chi practitioner's hands.

Grasp the Bird's Tail

Tutorial 3 @ 01.06

Don't be despondent if this posture takes a few lessons to master. Up to now you have been training in a linear fashion, this posture now brings its own challenges as we begin to face different aspects of the training room.

For directional teaching purposes identify a 'hook' in the room.

By this I mean using an item or location in the room to help everyone turn in the same direction, for example saying 'turn the torso towards the toy cupboard' (left), or 'turn the torso to the door' (right).

1. Keeping the fingers touching the pulse point, turn the hands over with the right hand palm up and the left hand palm down. At the same time fold at the waist, slightly lowering the hands in front of the body, with the elbow located in front of the Dantien (eyes looking at where the floor meets the wall).

Ensure that the weight is 95 per cent on the front foot and the back is straight from the heel to the hip to the shoulder, i.e. Wudang Sloping Stance.

Also remember, by turning the torso the hands will follow!

2. Drop the front toe and shift the weight forward, turning the torso which takes the hands to the left.

3. Turn the torso to the right (keeping the arms the same).

Tutorial 3 @ 01.20

1. Fold the knee and shift the body weight back. Drop the right elbow and take the hands slightly towards your right shoulder.

2. Turn the hands over and fold at the waist, slightly lowering the hands in front of the body. The left hand is now palm up and the right palm down.

3. Drop the front toe and shift the weight forward, turning the waist to the left, which takes the hands diagonally to the left.

Ensure the knees stay over the bridge of the foot.

ADD A STORY

Imagine there is a big bird in front of you (I have a peacock in my imagination – very Chinese). You are going to reach forward to try and 'grasp' the big bird by the tail. It shakes you off by turning (to your right), so you follow with your torso/hands – try again.

This time you manage to grasp a tail feather. You are going to pull it in towards your right shoulder, then turn your torso and fold slightly at the waist to pull it in front of you to the floor. Now turn and push it out of the window!

Single Whip – Forming a Bird's Beak

Single whip

Tutorial 3 @ 01.35

1. Shift the weight back slightly and bring in the right foot (45 degrees). Place the weight back onto the right foot.

   At the same time drop the right hand over the left with thumb and forefingers lightly touching to form a beak. Ensure the back of the hand is flat. (Note: the right hand finishes above the right knee.)

   Drop the right heel and sink into Horse Stance.

Tutorial 3 @ 01.53

2. Sinking into the right foot, step out with left foot (both feet should be in line) and touch the left toes to the floor.

VIP

Do not step too wide.

3. Sit into Horse Stance and settle the weight which should be even on both feet. Turn the torso to the left taking the hand with it. The left hand turns palm out (when above the left knee). Sink into the stance and settle. The upper body is facing forward and you should be looking at the back of the left hand.

To finish you can either go into Playing with the Dragon in the Clouds and repeat the Tai Chi Form or cross the hands to Close Form (see the following page).

Closing the Form

From Single Whip:

1. Extend the arms with both hands palm down.

2. Keep the knees relaxed with a slight hollow or bend in the back of the knees.

3. Take the weight onto the right foot, step up (slightly) with the left foot (both feet should now be under the hips). Fold the arms at the elbows, taking the hands in front of the body, left hand over right, palms facing down.

   As you unbend the knees, separate the hands and push them down the sides of the body. Stand upright, feet below hips, hips below shoulders, palms of the hands facing the floor and return to Ready Stance – relax.

Congratulations, you have now completed Tutorial 3 and the Tai Chi Form – feel *very* proud of yourself and your students.

CHI FOR CHILDREN

STRESS SURVIVAL

Sequence of Training

Shake Off Negativity

Chi Brushing

Building the Bridge

Qigong Exercises

Wood Qigong

Yin/Yang Hands

The Eagle

Tai Chi Form: Postures

Playing with the Dragon in the Clouds

About this Programme

This tutorial is for stressful situations. You can pull it out to use on its own when you need a 'quick fix'.

It is a short programme of techniques and exercises that will work if you are facing a stressful event. I have deliberately repeated some of the exercises and postures from previous tutorials because they are extremely good for calming purposes. Practised regularly they will help you and your students become calmer and more focused during tough times. However, I have also included some new techniques for you to try.

The techniques have been chosen specifically because they can improve concentration and reduce anxiety. This is particularly useful when practised prior to exams, interviews and so on.

As before, the techniques are based on the ancient Chinese arts of Tai Chi Chuan and Qigong. However, for the purpose of this tutorial we have included mind management techniques such as breathing techniques and subliminal reinforcement.

Repetition is the key to learning, so we recommend that you use some or all of the techniques from this programme on a regular basis. You have already learned some of them which will make learning easier. Use them daily for 10 to 15 minutes before, during and after exams, interviews or presentations. If you want a quick fix for stress and anxiety, use the whole tutorial. As we have recognized, when we look at mental wellbeing from a Chinese medicine perspective, fear inhibits learning and rational thoughts.

Anxiety

What are the Signs?

- Feeling fearful or a sense of panic.

- Feeling breathless, sweaty, or complaining of 'butterflies' or pains in the chest or stomach.

- Feeling tense, fidgety, using the toilet often.

- Poor concentration.

- Forgetfulness – blanking.

Confidence and self-esteem (or lack of) are a result of specific thought processes. However, we can reduce the debilitating type of anxiety by preparing in advance.

In today's environment it is recognized that children have to learn a wide range of tasks and skills throughout childhood.

Specialists and educationalists recognize that it is important for children to learn how to manage fear and/or anxiety, so that they behave appropriately and achieve.

If these negative emotions are present, it is important that children learn skills for coping more efficiently with their feelings. These emotions can inhibit confidence and prevent children from performing to the best of their ability, which could affect their future prospects.

The techniques in this tutorial work on a subconscious level, giving inner-peace and self-control. We wish to encourage a physical and psychological 'break with the past', to eliminate negativity, stress or fearfulness and to replace these feelings with positivity, confidence and calmness.

Discipline – E-bay

To remind you – discipline is a key component of Tai Chi and Qigong. This must be reflected in the way a class is run.

E-bay means *attention* and it is a good tool for bringing a class into line and letting the children know what you expect of them from the outset.

Calling your Students to Order

1. The teacher (Sifu) should clap his or her hands.

2. The students should firmly place one foot on the ground and then the other (not stamping), stand up straight, look at the teacher and say 'E-bay'.

3. They then stand to attention silently to wait for instructions.

In the days of martial law this would be used to pull together a large group of warriors and centre the mind for battle.

Breathing

Your mental state has a significant effect on breathing and the nervous system. When we are distressed or angry, our breathing becomes shallow and faster, and our heart rate also quickens. Some people may even sigh loudly (empty their lungs) in an effort to take in as much air as possible. This innate reaction is linked to our 'fight or flight' response and can result in hyperventilation, dizziness and in extreme cases fainting, which can create a feeling of anxiety. You may have experienced this at some point.

However, being aware of what is happening to us when we are emotionally challenged can help alleviate the symptoms. The ideal way is to breathe slowly and deeply, through the nose, using the diaphragm muscle, with a feeling of expanding the abdomen and dropping the breath – *do not force* the breath.

This technique is Nasal Breathing. If you suffer from nasal congestion, you or your students can breathe through the mouth.

Nasal Breathing

This is a very easy exercise to start with. It should be second nature to everyone in the room but the idea is to think about your breathing.

1. Breathe out slowly through your nose to empty your lungs (for a count of three). As your lungs empty your stomach muscles will tighten and your belly will flatten slightly.

2. Now relax the stomach muscles and breathe in fresh, clean air through the nose (for a count of two). Allowing the breath to sink naturally into your body, place your hands just below your belly button (lower Dantien) and feel your stomach swell.

3. Once your stomach feels full of air, empty your lungs once again by breathing out through the nose as before.

Repeat the process for several minutes; don't force the breath; be mindful and calm.

Please take care if you (or anyone doing this technique) have difficulties with breathing (asthma, bronchial problems, etc.). If so, you *must* count to three on the out breath and two on the in. (*If in doubt, please consult your doctor prior to undertaking this training.*)

The lower Dantien stores the power and helps ground (root) the Chi energy.

Managing the Mind

To complement the breathing, learn how to 'manage your mind' – guide the mind but do it gently.

Be in the moment (the here and now).

Count the breaths.

THE MANIC MONKEY

According to Chinese principles the mind is known as the Manic Monkey. When your mind wanders gently bring it back to the stillness and start counting again.

In the West this process is known as 'integrated awareness', the mind and body working together.

Shake Off Negativity

It is extremely important when facing important events to make a physical action to eliminate fear, which is a negative emotion.

You could utilize a visual aid to help lock out negativity. For example, make a mark on the inside of the door of the exam room (you could use the Yin/Yang symbol).

As you or your students close the door, press the mark (or symbol) to 'get rid of' negativity and 'seal in' a positive mental attitude.

Again, shake to disrupt feelings of negativity.

1. Allow your wrists to go limp and holding your elbows at shoulder height, shake your hands hard from side to side. Continue this for a count of 20. Now allow the shake to go down the body (a bit like a shiver) – shake the shoulders, shake the ribs, shake the hips, shake the knees *and*, as the singer Beyoncé would say, shake the 'booty'.

2. Lift one foot, shake it vigorously and then repeat with the other. You can hold onto a wall or the back of a chair for balance.

Or, shake the whole body to release any tension. This is fun!

Chi Brushing

VIP

Although we have already established an awareness of Chi, I feel it is so important that I want you to reflect on this subject to intensify your understanding. Remember, during training we want to get rid of the negative Chi and cultivate positive Chi.

Tutorial 4 @ 00.34

Once our Chi is flowing freely though our bodies we need to ensure that any negative Chi is banished and replaced with good, positive Chi. This is done by brushing away the old Chi.

This exercise can be done alone or in pairs (as before). However, please ensure that participants are happy with this hands-on technique.

During Tai Chi we want to encourage you to forget about the past (fear, problems, pressure from outside sources).

Remember: according to Chinese medicine fear blocks learning and could lead to learning problems.

Chi Brushing Yourself

1. Allow the left arm to hang down by your side in a relaxed manner.

2. With your right hand, brush firmly down the outside of the left arm and as you reach the end of the fingers pull off the old Chi and throw it onto the floor. (Do not throw it onto someone else as this is a bit like giving your horrible old cold to your friend – not very nice at all.)

3. Brush in a long sweep all the way down the outside of your left leg.

4. Brush the top of your foot and sweep all the old Chi onto the floor.

Now the other side.

Please ensure that your partner is happy with the following hands-on exercise. Ask if it's OK before you start and always treat your partner with respect.

Chi Brushing with a Partner

1. Stand behind your partner as they relax with their hands hanging down by their sides.

2. Take the palm of your left hand and place it on your partner's left shoulder – this is to ground yourself.

3. With the palm of your right hand brush across the shoulders left to right (as if you are brushing something off).

4. Keep your hand on your partner's shoulder and brush down the *outside* of their arm, over the hand and gently pull the old Chi from the tips of their fingers and throw it on the floor.

5. Run the palm of your right hand down the *outside* of their leg while still keeping your left hand on their shoulder. (Never impose yourself on your partner as this can be intimidating.) Brush the old Chi from their foot and onto the floor. (The hands on the shoulder can swap over to allow you to brush each leg, one at a time – it is quite tricky but you will be able to work it out easily enough.)

Repeat down the other side.

Swap places with your partner and repeat the exercise.

Now stop *quickly* – hold the hands under the Dantien, palms up, and lift to chest height, turn the hands over and push down to the Dantien.

When pushing down, encourage a feeling of settling and grounding the past (like coffee grains in a cafetière). Repeat as often as you wish.

The Dantien is located just below the tummy button. This is a centre to ground energy, according to Chinese medicine and martial arts.

Building the Bridge

VIP

If you teach only one thing, make it Building the Bridge.

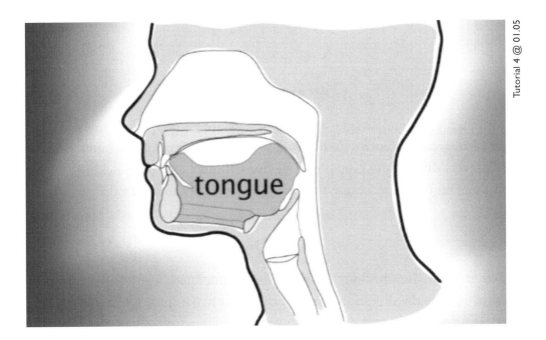

tongue

Tutorial 4 @ 01.05

Not only used in Tai Chi, this technique is widely recognized to drop you into a deep sense of calmness and to induce a state of meditation or mindfulness.

Touch the tip of your tongue to the roof of your mouth. Brush your tongue along the roof of your mouth and just behind the top teeth you come across a little indentation.

Gently press the tip of the tongue into the indentation and relax the jaw and teeth. Breathe in and out through the nose allowing the breath to drop to the abdomen slowly.

By doing this the Yin/Yang vessels are connected and the circuit is complete allowing the Chi to circulate around the body. This tongue touch is called Da Qiao (Building the Bridge), a technique which will drop you into a state of meditation, calm and relaxation.

Use this technique for any stressful event such as exams, interviews, presentations.

Do not build the bridge when driving.

Qigong Exercises

Although calm and simple, the movements are actually very powerful and move oxygen and energy (Chi) throughout all systems of the body, helping to prevent disease and promote longevity. Children are very quickly absorbed in these movements because they are easy to learn and fun to do.

Wood Qigong

The emotion for the liver is irritability (think livid/liver) and frustration, which affects the digestion, perhaps causing nausea and a feeling of unrest.

In your mind's eye (imagination) see a large strong oak tree, feel the strength of the tree entering the body and sinking to the feet while breathing in and out.

Stand with your feet directly under your hips, knees relaxed. Imagine that your feet are the roots of the strong oak tree and do not move from the ground.

The wood element relates to the liver (located beneath the right-hand side of your ribs). According to TCM the liver is the organ that relates to anger, frustration and other negative emotions. This exercise helps us expel the negative emotions while allowing positive energy (kindness) to develop.

1. Start this exercise in Ready Stance.

2. Curl the hands into a light fist (as though holding a baby bird) and rest the forearms on the hips, relaxing the shoulders.

3. Push one hand forward, and turn the fist to push with the hand, palm forwards, as if pushing something away from you. Extend the arm in front of you with the other tucked into your waist.

4. Slowly swap positions, pulling the extended arm in and pushing the other out. Coordinate the palm change as the hands pass each other in a smooth movement.

As you push, breathe out and make the steam train noise, 'Shhhhh'. Feel the waist turning as you push and pull.

You can encourage your students to do this exercise facing a friend or partner, which is initially exciting. Then ask your students to stop talking, Build the Bridge and eventually close their eyes. This is very hypnotic.

Some students may relate this to Karate, therefore it is *essential* that the exercise is practised slowly and the Laogong points (in the centre of the palm) face each other as the hands pass each other.

Encourage your students to feel that they are activating a laser beam that points from one Laogong point (in the palm of one hand to the other). Or imagine you are polishing a large emerald to make it shine, or turning on a laser beam that is radiating from the palm of one hand to the other. Perhaps you can hear the laser beam? This is a controlling technique, allowing the students to take control of their emotions, such as anger and frustration and replacing their negative emotions with positive feelings and kindness.

This Qigong is accompanied by a sound. On the out-breath make a low, comforting 'Shhhhhh', similar to a steam train or the wind blowing through the trees. Make no sound on the in-breath.

Yin/Yang Hands

By adopting the Tai Chi philosophy of opposites, Yin and Yang, this technique benefits the brain by improving blood flow and spurring cell growth.

Standing or sitting, cross the hands in front of the body, hands palm in. The *front* hand will always finish facing the back of the room.

1. Cross the hands in front of the chest, palms facing inwards, right hand outside of left.

2. Drop both hands down and out, in a stretch finishing with the right-hand palm facing backwards and the left-hand palm facing forwards. Gently turn the head to look at the hand that is facing backwards.

3. Bring the hands back in front of the chest, palms facing inwards, left hand outside of right hand.

4. Drop both hands down and out, in a stretch finishing with the right-hand palm facing forwards, left-hand palm facing backwards (the opposite of the last time). Turn the head to look at the hand that is facing backwards.

This exercise demonstrates Yin and Yang. It takes a lot of concentration and encourages relaxation – it's hard to do if you are trying too hard!

The Eagle

For most Qigong exercises you keep the eyelids relaxed, as this helps to sense the energy and visualize without distraction.

However, when you need to concentrate on balance, the best solution is to keep your eyes open and focus on a point straight ahead of you. This exercise is also easier to do when the body is very relaxed, so don't make it the first one in your routine.

The Eagle is excellent for improving your immune system. According to Chinese medicine, overthinking and worry depletes the immune system leading to coughs and chest complaints. A lot of students come to the exam room with respiratory problems; this could be alleviated by practising The Eagle!

Tutorial 4 @ 03.30

1. Take up the Qigong standing posture, ensuring that you feel balanced with your centre of gravity over a point just behind the balls of your feet, known as the Bubbling Well.

2. Bring your hands in front of your body, palms facing inwards and your fingers spread open, as if holding the Chi ball. Always maintain a feeling of roundness in your arms.

3. Slowly draw your hands out to your sides, opening the chest, palms of the hands facing down.

4. Looking straight ahead, drop the elbows and form the hands into the bird's beak. While doing this, keep the back straight and chin drawn slightly backwards (the head should feel suspended from the ceiling, as if being supported by a piece of silver thread, and the neck is relaxed).

5. As you pull your arms into this position, lift your heels off the floor and balance on the balls of your feet. Engage your intent by concentrating on a fixed spot directly in front of you.

Now visualize that you are a great eagle flying through the air. Your arms are your wings and the sun is warming them. Hold the position for a few seconds.

6. Bring your arms down, open the hands to form feathers on the end of the eagle's wings! Drop the elbows, and then lower the arms to the starting position. At the same time place your heels back on the ground. While you are doing this exercise, breathe deeply but naturally.

Repeat the sequence four to six times – *enjoy*.

Tai Chi Form: Postures

The essence of Tai Chi is to be totally engaged, not thinking about the last move or the next, but concentrating purely on where you are. This is known as being 'in the moment'.

Playing with the Dragon in the Clouds

This is a calming exercise that is practised in smooth 'wave like' movements. It is designed to promote rhythmical breathing and relaxation.

We are going to count some of the movements in Cantonese, a dialect used mainly in Southern China. You will be counting Yat where you see 1, Yee where you see 2 and San where you see 3.

1 = Yat
2 = Yee
3 = San

Start this exercise in Horse Stance.

Playing with the dragon in the clouds

Tutorial 1 @ 09.27

1. Hold your arms up in front of you with your hands, palms out, at shoulder height. (Note: if your hands were to drop they would land on your lap.)

2. Turn the torso (upper body) and drop your left hand in front of your tummy (palm in), then bring it round in front of the body, until it meets and is in front of your right hand (which has remained where it started).

   You should now have your left hand in front of your right hand, as if holding a ball. At this point imagine you have a dragon between your hands and you are holding its tail.

3. From this position bring the right hand down in a similar swoop and slowly turn from the torso to bring the left hand, palm out, back across at chin level, right hand, palm in, at tummy level.

   The hands will face each other, as if holding a ball on the left-hand side of the body. You are now holding the dragon's head.

Keep going, concentrating on the movement, and we will now add mindful techniques to this posture to enhance the outcome.

As you repeat this movement, breathe in and out through the nose allowing the breath to fall and the abdomen to expand, as in the breathing exercise.

For the younger age group engage the mind by using the imagination. Guide the student to paint a story by asking questions about their dragon.

We know that everyone's dragon is different because we have already designed our own special, protecting dragon. In fact we even painted it a special colour.

Now is the time for you to take out your dragon, the 'one you prepared earlier'. See him or her radiate in your own magic Chi colour. Stretch out your dragon and feel calm, protected and full of confidence.

Calming Techniques

You can now guide your students through the calming techniques to 'layer your sheets of learning' (rice paper) one on top of the other!

- Lightly breathe in and out through your nose.
- Feel your tummy expand with the breath.
- Build the Bridge (tip of tongue to roof of mouth).
- How does your dragon feel?

To finish, you could follow Closing and Some Fun techniques described in Tutorial 1 (page 73).

FURTHER TECHNIQUES AND REMINDERS

Techniques to Try Any Time

These techniques have been documented in ancient Chinese cave drawings and continue to be widely practised to this day.

Ten Dragons Running through the Forest

This technique helps to release tension in the scalp/head.

Guide all ten fingers through the hair from the front hairline. Zig zag the fingers over the top of the head and down the neck.

Repeat as often as you like.

Shake out the hands (onto the floor).

Knocking on Heaven's Gate

This technique helps to wake up the brain.

Cup ears with the palms of the hands with the fingers on the occipital point (back of the head).

Using the fingertips, tap with gusto, evenness and briskness all across, up, down and around the rear of the skull to wake up the brain.

Do *not* practise Knocking on Heaven's Gate if you (or your students) have inner ear problems, grommets and the like.

The Old Man and the Tide Pool

This is an excellent Qigong for the younger student.

This Qigong is accompanied by sounds generated to expel stagnant Chi and negative energy, encouraging positivity. You will be familiar with this process as the sounds are practised in the same way as the Five Element Qigong sounds. Do not shout!

(Utilizing sounds within a technique is not applicable to all Qigong exercises, however it is relevant to this one.)

Do not do this Qigong if you have high *or* low blood pressure.

Start the exercise by standing in Qigong Ready Stance.

1. Take a deep breath in to the Dantien (located at the tummy button) and imagine the lungs expanding and filling with a bright white light.

2. While inhaling stretch both arms out to the side of the body.

3. Bend over (to a comfortable level) and start to exhale making a 'Shhhhh' sound. At the same time imagine old stagnant Chi rushing down the arms and flowing into the ground.

Swing or swish both arms from side to side, crossing the arms in the middle (as if rippling the hands in a pond).

1. Slowly come back to an upright position while imagining droplets of grey water or steam flowing off the end of the fingers.

2. Breathe in, look upwards, and raise the hands above the head and in your mind's eye see a bright white light filling the chest.

3. Now exhale half of your breath, pulling both hands (palms out) to shoulder level, and make the sound 'Haaaaa'.

4. Exhale the second half of your breath, turning the hands into soft fists (as if holding a baby bird) and dropping them down to the hips, and make the sound 'Whoooo'.

   Repeat the last three steps (2, 3 and 4) three times. This equals one set. Repeat the full set a minimum of three times.

When teaching younger participants it is sometimes too much to expect them to be able to perform steps 3 and 4 on one exhale. At such times, I instruct them to inhale after the 'Haaaaaa' and before the 'Whoooo'.

The following story is associated with this ancient Qigong:

One night, on a full moon, an old man on the southern coast of China went looking for fish to feed his family. Holding his lamp up he gazed down into a beautiful clear pond and saw a large silver coin at the bottom of the tide pool. 'Oh my,' he exclaimed, 'look at that silver! With a silver coin that size, I could retire and my family would live in luxury.'

So the old man stretched his arms wide and began splashing his hands in the tide pool, trying to grasp the huge coin. 'Shhhhhh' went the water, as the old man tried to grab at nothing. Frustrated, the old man looked up, reaching into the night sky and his eyes widened as he saw the full moon. 'Haaaaa,' exclaimed the old man, 'it's the moon.' 'Whooo,' cried the old man, 'it's only the reflection of the moon on the pool – there is no money!'

Ground your Energy

It is very important to ground your energy at the end of each Qigong/ Tai Chi session. This is very simple to do: just place your hands over your Dantien, located just below your tummy button. Breathe in and out and drop all of your thought down to your hands. This is to ground your Chi, as you don't want to finish a session of Tai Chi with your Chi/your students Chi stuck up in the head.

This is Earth position and we should lead the mind to feel that we are sinking into soft earth with a feeling of connectivity to the world, grounding the thoughts in our head.

As you breathe in, draw your mind's eye to the Dantien.

Respect – Gung Fu

Tutorial 4 @ 05.40

Respect is an extremely important part of Chinese teaching and this is also reflected in Tai Chi.

At the end of a class, teacher and students should show respect to each other in the form of a physical and vocal acknowledgement.

Gung Fu means good (or hard) work and when said to another is accompanied by the following gesture of respect.

1. Take the left hand in front of the chest palm facing to the right.

2. The right hand forms a soft fist and is rested into the palm of the left hand.

3. Now bow slightly at the waist to show respect for the good work that students and teacher have done.

The Importance of Relaxation

Relaxation is extremely important although often difficult to achieve. When we are in a state of relaxation we encourage deep abdominal breathing to take place. This results in more oxygen being pumped around the body.

Relaxation can also help to lower blood pressure.

The following exercise will improve circulation.

I am repeating the following exercise because it is very important to ground energy when you have finished practising Tai Chi and/or Qigong, otherwise energy gets 'stuck' in the head. I have experienced this as a thumping headache.

Chi Brushing to Close

At the beginning we brushed the old/stagnant Chi off and grounded it by throwing it onto the floor. With this exercise we now want to close all the new/energized Chi. This is similar to a 'warm-down'.

1. Allow the left arm to hang down by your side, in a relaxed manner.

2. With your right hand brush firmly *down* the left arm and as you reach the end of the fingers run your hand *up* the inside of the arm.

3. Place your left hand on your right shoulder and run down the outside of the arm and up the inside.

4. Place your hands on your ribs (just under armpits), bend gently and continue to run your hands down the outside of the ribs, hips and legs.

5. Brush your hands round the front of your feet and run the hands up the inside of the legs until you reach the inside of your knees.

6. Slowly stand up – the last point to come up is the head. Now rest your hands over the Dantien area.

Stand quietly for a minute or so to allow the Chi to settle down. This is to avoid the Chi getting 'stuck' in your head which could cause headaches.

Thank you for using this resource. I hope that you have found it informative and now go on to work with others, sharing your knowledge.

Take your time teaching these techniques. Keep it simple by picking out a couple of easy exercises and learn them well before you try to teach them to someone else. The secret is to keep going. In time this will all become easier – I promise.

Encourage your students to help you as you are also 'new to the subject'. Empowering others always produces lots of enthusiasm.

'Every day the teacher repeats those actions that lead to understanding. Chop wood, carry water, every day. Without routine/repetition there is no learning. Without surprise there is no wisdom.' (Lao Tzu, *Tao Te Ching*)

Testimonials

Barlby School Sport Partnership, North Yorkshire

The Chi for Children programme, delivered by UK Tai Chi, has made a huge impact within the Barlby School Sport Partnership.

After a comprehensive review of the partnership's activities, it became apparent that young people wanted more from their current physical education programme. There was also a real need to target those children that took little or no interest in the traditional team activities that were currently being offered.

Alongside this the School Sport Partnership wanted to run an initiative that not only captured the imagination of all the young people involved but offered primary teaching staff the opportunity to gain a qualification in delivery, achieved through an excellent personalised mentoring scheme offered by UK Tai Chi.

The impact to date has been huge. Twenty primary schools (45% of all schools) have been involved with the Chi for Children initiative, with over 20 teachers attending the Train the Trainer Module 1. Over 200 pupils now regularly participate in Tai Chi either in the classroom as a focus session or as a stand-alone PE lesson. One school was even used as a showpiece example in the Partnership Dance Platform event.

As well as the health and physical benefits to all the young people, what has been most encouraging is the impact the initiative has had within the whole school. Schools have been using Tai Chi as a means of stress relief for pupils (and staff) prior to exams, as a means of calming children down after lunchtimes, as a way of focusing children in the mornings to start the day.

On the whole the programme has been a huge success and we are really pleased with both the impact it has had within our schools and the professionalism in which it has been delivered by UK Tai Chi.

Andy Clay
Partnership Development Manager
Barlby School Sport Partnership, Selby, North Yorkshire

Saltaire Primary School, Yorkshire

Hi Betty

When we last spoke you asked for some feedback on the impact of Tai Chi on the children, especially Y6 in the run up to tests. We are fortunate in having Chris[11] who is such a good Tai Chi teacher. In order to prepare children for the tests we wanted them to be alert and to reduce some of their anxiety. I watched Chris lead the sessions, the result of which was the children looked relaxed, alert and ready to focus. During the sessions the children were really engaged and concentrated their minds and bodies on the exercises. With the music playing in the background it looked very impressive.

Kind Regards
Kevin Keogan
Head Teacher
Saltaire Primary School
Shipley, Yorkshire

Fairburn Community Primary School

Great North Road, Fairburn,
Knottingley, West Yorkshire,
WF11 9JY
Head teacher: Miss E. Brown

Betty has been working with us in school during the last year. I instigated Tai Chi sessions in school after we had a family join the school who were suffering severe domestic abuse. Rather than implement a host of intervention programmes, it seemed more important that the children gained a sense of security and calmness which Tai Chi has undoubtedly helped provide.

Staff joined in the weekly sessions over a period of a term. We now have a TA [teaching assistant] who has trained as a Tai Chi leader and all children from both Key Stage One and Two have regular sessions. It has been enthusiastically received by staff, parents and children and is now an established part of not only the PE curriculum but is also helping us to fulfil the Learning to be Healthy aspect of the Every Child Matters Framework.

As a result of Tai Chi sessions, it is noticeable that the children are calmer and more focused. They also find it fun!

---

11 Chris Evans, Teaching Assistant, is part of the train-the-trainer programme now successfully delivering Tai Chi to kids in the school, and in the local community.

GLOSSARY

Abdominals   Muscle group that support the torso.

ADHD   Attention deficit hyperactivity disorder.

Aerobic   'With oxygen', exercises that increase the intake of oxygen.

British Council for Chinese Martial Arts (BCCMA)   Governing body for Tai Chi in Great Britain.

British Open Championships   Tai Chi competition held yearly in Great Britain.

Bruce Lee   Popularized Chinese martial arts through movies, the forerunner to Jackie Chan and Jet Lee.

Bubbling Well   A point located on the sole of each foot, behind the ball of the foot, in line with the second toe. Stimulating this point promotes calmness and encourages the flow of Chi.

Building the Bridge   Technique for calming the mind.

Cantonese   One of the dialects used in China.

Chi   Energy or breath work.

Chi Brushing   Exercise to circulate Chi.

Chi for Children   Programme of Tai Chi/Qigong for children.

Chinese healthcare   Traditional Chinese Medicine (TCM).

Core structure   Large muscle group in the body.

Curtsey to the Queen   Tai Chi posture.

Dantien (lower)   Physical centre of gravity/a place to store energy.

Dojo   Training room.

E-bay   Call to attention.

Enter the Dragon   Famous movie featuring Bruce Lee.

Fight or flight   A physiological response to acute stress.

145

Five Winds School of Tai Chi Chuan   Exemplary school of Tai Chi Chuan in Scotland, UK.

Form   Sequence of Tai Chi postures.

Frame   Range of motion in which Tai Chi is practised.

Golden Cockerel   Posture from Tai Chi Form.

Grasp the Bird's Tail   Posture from Tai Chi Form.

Grounding energy   Connecting thoughts (movement) to the ground.

Guard   Defensive posture from Tai Chi Form.

Gung Fu   In this context meaning good or hard work.

Holding the Golden Plate   Posture from Tai Chi Form.

Holistic   All aspects of our wellbeing – psychological, physical, social.

Immune system   Natural defence system of the body.

Inhibition   Holding back a natural impulse.

Integrated awareness   Mindfulness.

Jackie Chan   Martial arts movie star born in Hong Kong in 1954.

Jet Lee   Martial arts movie star born in Beijing, China in 1963.

Karate   Japanese martial art.

Kata   Specific series of movements practised in Japanese martial arts.

Knocking on Heaven's Gate   Technique for improving brain activity.

Kung Fu   Generic name for Chinese martial arts.

Laying down sheets of rice paper   Description of how we teach Tai Chi.

Li Shou   Chinese term for light top/heavy bottom.

Mandarin   A Chinese dialect.

Manic Monkey   A busy state of mind.

Master   Someone who is in control.

Meditation   Practice to calm the mind.

Meridians   The body's natural energy channels.

Mind's eye   Imagination.

Mirror image   As if facing a mirror/your reflection.

Nasal Breathing   Way of breathing in Tai Chi.

Planting the Feet on the Ground   A Qigong.

Playing with the Dragon in the Clouds   Posture in Tai Chi Form.

Polish Palms   A Qigong.

Pulling the Bow   A Qigong.

Qigong   Chinese exercises to improve health.

Rice paper   Very thin paper made from the rice plant.

Rumble   Low rolling noise used in the Five Element Qigongs.

Sea Bottom   Perineum – point at the base of the pelvis where the Yin and Yang channels meet.

Seven Stars   Posture in Tai Chi Form.

Shoulder's Nest   Part of body between upper arm and clavicle or collar bone.

Sifu/Shifu   Teacher/tutor or father.

Silver thread   Pulled up from the top of the head.

Single Whip   Posture in Tai Chi Form.

Snake Creeps Down   Posture in Tai Chi Form.

Spreading the Wings   Posture in Tai Chi Form.

Tai Chi Chuan   Supreme, ultimate, fist.

Tai Chi classics   Ancient instructions followed in Tai Chi.

Tai Chi Union for Great Britain (TCUGB)   Union for Tai Chi in Great Britain.

Taijiquan   Pinyin (the official system to transcribe Chinese characters) meaning Tai Chi Chuan.

The Eagle   A Qigong.

The Old Man and the Tide Pool   A Qigong.

Tiger's Claw   Hand position in Qigong to develop strength in the hand.

Tiger's Mouth   The 'publicue' flap of skin between thumb and forefinger.

Torso   The trunk or body (excluding the arms and legs).

Traditional Chinese Medicine or TCM   A way of healthcare in China.

UK Tai Chi   A leading provider of Tai Chi training in the UK.

Ward off   To push away – a technique of defence in Tai Chi.

Working within the moment   Meditation or mindfulness.

Wudang   Mountain range in China where Tai Chi Chuan was discovered. also means 'martial duty' and a style of Tai Chi.

Wudang stance   Martial stance used in Tai Chi.

Yee Chin Ching   Physical exercises practised in China for postural alignment and conditioning.

Yellow Emperor   Legendary Chinese leader and hero.

Yin/Yang   A Taoist symbol that represents polar opposites.

Yin/Yang Hands   Exercise to engage the mind.

RESOURCES

Some information in this resource is the work of others. I would like to acknowledge their work below.

References

Five Winds School of Tai Chi Chuan

www.five-winds.co.uk

Stasguide

www.satsguide.co.uk

Brain Gym

www.braingym.org.uk

Further Reading

The Practice of Wudang Tai Chi Chuan by Ian Cameron
Golden Horse Classics, UK

The Practice of Wudang Tai Chi Chuan – Tai Chi Weapons Forms by Ian Cameron
Golden Horse Classics, UK

The Way of Qigong by Kenneth S. Cohen
Ballantyne Books, New York

Take Time by Mary Nash-Wortham and Jean Hunt
The Robinson Press, England

Chi for Children Word Search

A	E	P	G	Y	K	N	H	H	E	A	R	T	E	D
D	S	A	E	K	Y	I	N	T	Q	U	Y	P	B	X
B	R	C	Y	D	L	I	E	F	A	I	S	O	A	I
U	S	A	V	I	C	K	N	D	B	U	N	P	Y	R
I	C	L	G	H	T	H	N	G	E	S	N	A	K	E
L	C	D	V	O	P	U	U	D	Y	A	M	Y	T	R
D	O	B	H	H	N	T	G	S	T	A	O	S	P	L
I	C	E	G	N	Y	K	L	S	I	C	N	N	N	I
N	K	R	T	S	Y	H	M	F	J	P	I	G	E	V
G	E	E	C	T	P	P	T	R	K	Y	I	N	W	E
T	R	K	E	T	A	I	C	H	I	D	Y	R	Z	R
H	E	E	P	H	C	Y	A	P	W	E	B	Y	C	N
E	L	T	C	H	I	A	N	I	N	X	B	E	N	U
B	T	V	R	U	O	O	T	D	H	A	T	Q	Y	P
R	Y	T	D	W	A	T	I	Q	I	G	O	N	G	U
I	S	W	H	E	R	K	O	I	E	E	F	O	M	N
D	U	A	O	A	L	L	P	T	S	T	H	C	O	R
G	T	T	H	O	N	D	F	O	P	K	M	Y	I	I
E	U	E	K	E	D	A	N	P	L	L	O	J	E	H
E	A	R	T	H	W	K	U	Q	E	L	N	A	N	C
V	K	E	U	T	A	I	F	M	E	D	K	E	J	I
W	E	O	D	A	F	I	R	E	N	B	E	S	S	A
S	S	L	R	N	G	W	O	T	K	U	Y	I	A	T
L	U	N	G	S	I	S	R	A	T	T	M	N	E	K
J	Y	N	G	S	O	N	R	L	Y	J	F	J	I	U

Find the following words in the words search:

YIN YANG	COCKEREL	WATER
BUILDING THE BRIDGE	CHI	QIGONG
TAI CHI	KIDNEY	EBAY
UK TAI CHI	METAL	HEART
DRAGON	FIRE	LIVER
SNAKE	EARTH	LUNGS
MONKEY	WOOD	SPLEEN

The answers are on the next page.[12]

---

12 Thanks to Steph Parkin for this excellent resource.

Answers to Word Search

							H	E	A	R	T	E
D					Y							B
B	R					I						A
U		A				N						Y
I			G					S	N	A	K	E
L	C			O				Y				
D	O				N			A				L
I	C								N			I
N	K									G		V
G	E											E
T	R			T	A	I	C	H	I	Y		R
H	E							E				
E	L		C	H	I			N				
B							D					
R						I	Q	I	G	O	N	G
I	W				K							
D	A	O					S					
G	T		O				P		M			I
E	E			D			L		O			H
E	A	R	T	H			E		N			C
						M	E		K			I
				F	I	R	E	N	E			A
							T		Y			T
L	U	N	G	S			A					K
							L					U

Yin and Yang Spinner

Watch the symbols in the circle constantly rotate

Cut out the symbol, pierce a hole in the centre, and push a straw through. Twirl the straw and watch the Yin and Yang rotate.

Personal Development Chart for Teachers

Tai Chi

www.uktaichi.com

Training contributes to a number of the professional standards for teachers recognized by Ofsted (*Office for Standards in Education in the UK*), in particular Q1, Q2, Q8, Q10, and Q14.

The aim of the training is to offer Tai Chi as a complement to the more formal examples of physical education to empower adults and children to value good physical health and mental wellbeing.

Comments from previous course evaluation: 'An excellent and inspirational course.' 'I hope to introduce aspects of Tai Chi into the school curriculum to aid children's concentration.'

Teachers name:

School/Club/Youth Group:

Training (length of training time for each tutorial):

Comments:

Signed/date:

Teacher* QTS requirements	Helping children to achieve (demonstrate learning)	Tutorial 1 The Basics (10 weeks)	Comments:	Signed/date:
Q1, Q2 Establish positive relationship with children	Programme meets diverse needs (physiological and psychological)	Demonstrate understanding of benefits of Five Element Qigong and relevance to education and your teaching		
	Teacher and students collaborate Establish positive relationships	Demonstrate proficiency in teaching Five Element Qigong Discuss outcomes Empower students to teach others		
	Promote students Health and Safety and wellbeing	Review risk assessment and individual needs Discuss need for discipline and respect		

*Qualified Teacher Status

Communicate effectively with young people, colleagues, parents and carers	Build confidence and self-esteem Help, listen and respect others	Teacher to demonstrate proficiency in teaching Tutorial 1 Chi for Children Students to help teach others Playing with the Dragon and understanding respect by using Gung Fu
		Tutorial 2 Centring and Balancing (10 weeks)
Q8 Teacher open to wider/ innovative teaching methods	Chi for Children is an innovative programme bringing together traditional training and contemporary teaching methods	Teacher to reflect and evaluate value of innovative methods such as Chi for Children and demonstrate proficiency in teaching more technical aspects of programme
Demonstrate the positive values, attitudes and behaviour expected from young people	Establish ability to watch, listen and follow instructions. Work as an individual and with a partner, showing respect to each other	Demonstrate proficiency in teaching Tai Chi Form from Step Back and Push the Monkey to Holding the Golden Plate finishing with Curtsey to the Queen
		20 weeks total
		Tutorial 3 Opening the Form (10 weeks)
		Be proficient in teaching Tai Chi Form from Opening the Form to Single Whip

Q10 Have knowledge and understanding of a range of teaching, learning and behaviour strategies	Recognise students diverse needs to overcome potential learning barriers	Final assessment: Demonstrate teaching from Opening the Form to Closing the Form Discuss outcomes with your students and how you can help them succeed (and in return recognize your own skills)	
Set realistic targets for children		Involve students in every aspect of learning Chi for Children Take 'bite size pieces' of learning and learn gradually	

30 weeks total

Tutorial 4 Stress Survival

Have a secure knowledge and understanding of subject	Personalize learning and provide opportunities for learners to achieve their potential	Review practices Assess, monitor and feedback: Review teaching methods Support and guide students to reflect on their learning Identify progress and learning needs	Additional resources: Brain Gym Take Time
Recognize how Chi for Children relates to other educational resources and benefits to school, etc.	E.g. Every Child Matters: 5 outcomes young people have identified as key to their wellbeing both in childhood and later in life: Being healthy, staying safe, enjoying and achieving, making a positive contribution and achieving economic wellbeing	Core skills gained from participating in Educational Tai Chi/Qigong 'Chi for Children'	Initiatives: *Healthy Schools* *Every Child Matters**

* *Every Child Matters* and *Healthy Schools* are a set of government reforms in the UK supported by the Children Act 2004, see www.education.gov.uk.

Questionnaire for Students

School/group name: _____

Leader's name: _____

Today's date: _____

Comments:

_____

	Strongly Agree	Agree	Disagree	Strongly Disagree

Please tick underneath the symbol that you agree with the most

I sometimes feel worried/anxious				
I sometimes feel under a lot of pressure which can make me angry				
Sometimes my emotions erupt!				
I find it hard to concentrate when I feel stressed				
I often feel I could do better if I knew how to calm myself down				
During Tai Chi I feel in control of my emotions				
During and after doing Tai Chi I feel nice and calm				
After doing Tai Chi I feel that I have lots of energy				

INDEX